Gayle A. Soucek

Doves

Everything About Housing, Health, Nutrition, and Breeding

Filled with Full-color Photographs
Illustrations by Michele Earle-Bridges

BARRON'S

2 CONTENTS

INTRODUCTION TO DOVES

Humans have had a special affinity for birds as far back as history can trace. Over the ages, birds have been kept as companions, hunted or raised as food, and viewed as messengers of the gods.

Perhaps no other species has enjoyed such a long and richly symbolic relationship with humankind as those of the *Columbidae* family, which is comprised of more than 300 species of doves and pigeons.

Doves appear in the revelations and writings of most religions and in the folk tales and mythology of almost every culture. In Christianity, doves are frequently used as a symbol of the Holy Spirit. In the Bible, a dove returned to Noah bearing an olive branch as proof that the waters of the Great Flood were receding from Earth. In Greek mythology, a dove led Jason and the Argonauts safely between the treacherous Symplegades, or Clashing Islands, at the mouth of the Black Sea. In return, the goddess Minerva placed the constellation Columba in the sky to honor the dove's bravery. In European folk

Gentle and quiet, doves are the perfect pet for many people.

traditions, a dove circling the home of a dying person means that the individual's soul will rest in peace. Even a brief scan of literature shows that the image of a dove has become synonymous in most cultures with peace, gentleness, harmony, and marital fidelity.

Traits

These images reflect many of the real-life traits that make doves so attractive as pets. They are usually docile and gentle birds that are hardy and require less complicated care than many other species of pet birds. Their normally peaceful nature, quiet demeanor, and relative ease of maintenance make them an especially good choice for a first-time bird owner. They are long-lived, with a life span that can exceed 20 years with proper care, so you can look forward to many years of companionship. They are great pets even for young children, provided an adult supervises the care and feeding. Because they are quiet birds, they are suitable for apartment dwellers that might not be able to keep a noisy parrot. For all these reasons and more, no wonder that doves are some of the most popular companion birds in captivity!

Doves vs. Pigeons

Although doves and pigeons are in the same family, and the names are often used interchangeably, there are some differences. Doves are usually smaller and sleeker, whereas pigeons tend to be larger, stockier birds, although there are exceptions to this rule. This book will concentrate on the most commonly kept pet dove species, primarily the Diamond Dove (*Geopelia cuneata)* and the Ringneck Dove (*Streptopelia risoria).*

Although some larger doves and pigeons can make wonderful companions, they require much more space and room to fly. As a result, their housing and husbandry needs are quite different from the small doves, which are suitable as house pets. For the sake of simplicity, the term *dove* will be used throughout the book, although in most instances the information given applies equally to the larger species generally referred to as pigeons.

Anatomy

No matter what their size, all doves and pigeons share common physical traits. They are muscular birds with short necks and heads that appear small in relation to their bodies.

Beaks: Dove beaks are short and narrow, with a slightly curved tip. They have the unusual ability to drink by sucking water up through their beaks like a straw, without tipping their heads back to swallow like most other birds. The beak is relatively soft at its base and hardens toward the tip.

Legs and toes: Their legs are relatively short and clearly scaled, with strong feet and nails. Their toes are anisodactyl, which means that three toes point forward and one points backward. This is in contrast to the zygodactyl toes of parrots, owls, and woodpeckers, which are arranged as two toes forward and two toes backward.

Doves in the Wild

Doves and pigeons are a wide-ranging group, varying in size from about 6 inches (15 cm) or less to a few very large species that might reach 33 inches (84 cm) in length.

Diversity: Doves and pigeons can be found on every continent except Antarctica. The largest diversity occurs throughout Australasia and the Pacific Islands. Approximately 14 species are found in North America, although some of these have been introduced and are not indigenous to the continent.

Groupings: In general, doves are divided into two groups: seed eaters and fruit eaters. Fruit-eating doves are beautiful, but are difficult to maintain in captivity and are not suited as pets. In later chapters, some of these exotic species will be discussed, but all common pet doves will fall into the seed-eating group.

Vocalization

Doves are relatively quiet birds, whose vocalizations are limited mostly to a variety of soft, low-pitched cooing sounds. Even though they are much quieter than most other cage birds, keep in mind that their cooing is persistent and repetitive, which might become annoying to a very sensitive person. Most people, however, find the gentle calls soothing and pleasant.

Breeding

Doves are quick to mature, with some species sexually mature by about six months of age. In spite of their early maturity, they can be long-lived, up to 20 years or more. This is, of course, something you must consider before you bring a dove into your life. These are not short-lived "disposable" pets. They are monogamous, and some will mate for life.

They are not particularly talented or creative nest builders. Most dove nests are a loose arrangement of twigs and grasses placed on a flat surface, such as a tree branch or ledge. Captive-bred doves will nest happily in commercially available canary nests, food dishes, flowerpots, small shallow baskets, or simply on the cage floor. The hen lays one or two glossy white eggs (pale brown in a few species), which hatch after an incubation period of 11–30 days, depending on the species.

Dove hatchlings are altricial. This means they are born blind, mostly naked (with just sparse down), and totally helpless and dependent upon the parents for food and warmth. The parents take turns feeding the young with a crop milk that is unique to pigeons and doves. In most bird species with altricial chicks, parent birds feed regurgitated food. In pigeon and dove species, however, both parents produce a high-protein slurry of crop cells, fluids, and partially digested food to feed their chicks. The young usually fledge and are ready to leave the nest as early as 10 days or as long as 4 weeks, depending on the species.

Common Pet Species

As mentioned earlier, this book concentrates on the common and easy to care for Ringneck and Diamond Doves. You might run across a few other species being sold as pets. Most of the information included in this book will apply to those species as well, but proceed cautiously. Research the species you are considering, and be certain you are aware of any special needs in husbandry and nutrition. Some less-common doves have very specific requirements and will not do well if those needs are ignored. Most reputable breeders will not sell exotic doves into the pet trade without first making sure that they are going to an experienced aviculturist. Ultimately, though, you must take the responsibility to provide properly for your new pet.

Diamond Doves

Diamond Doves (*Geopelia cuneata)* are small, seed-eating doves that are well established in the pet trade. These Australian natives are diminutive, about 7½ inches (19 cm) long and weighing about an ounce (29 g) or less. They are peaceful and hardy, and they make a wonderful choice for beginners. The normal coloration is brownish gray to gray with a creamy white abdomen and conspicuous white flecks or diamonds across the wings. Adults have a bright coral-colored eye ring and orange irises. Their beaks are olive brown, and their feet and legs are flesh colored. In addition to normals, about 17 color mutations are now available, including white, silver, yellow, cinnamon, and pied.

Diamond Doves are affectionate and gentle. They do best when kept in pairs. One can be kept as a single pet, but be prepared to offer it a lot of attention and interaction. If you want

The Diamond Dove is one of the smallest dove species and can live quite happily in an indoor cage.

Less common members of the dove family, such as this Bronze-winged pigeon, need more specialized care and larger accommodations.

Large doves and pigeons do best in outdoor planted aviaries.

Bleeding-Heart pigeons, named for the patch of red feathers on their breasts, require a varied diet of fruit, seeds, and insects.

Even in large aviaries, it is important not to crowd the birds or problems such as disease and aggression can occur.

TIP

Cautionary Note

A loose domestic dove is helpless and vulnerable outdoors. It will not survive for long. Tame doves will not know how to hunt for food, will not have the skills to evade predators, and will most likely be bullied severely by wild birds.

If for any reason you must give up your pet dove, *never* release it into the wild. Not only is doing so a cruel death sentence, but it is also illegal. With few exceptions, doves are considered nonindigenous species, which means they do not occur naturally in the wild in the United States. The release of nonindigenous species into the wild can pose a severe threat to indigenous wildlife and plant life, and the U.S. Fish and Wildlife Service takes a very dim view of this indeed. If you cannot keep your pet, contact a shelter, local bird club, or even a veterinarian's office for advice. Euthanizing the bird would be more humane than to release it to starve or be killed by predators.

to keep the birds in pairs but do not want breeding to occur, two birds of the same sex will usually live together happily if they are put together when they are still very young or if they are allowed to get to know each other slowly. In a large aviary, they can be kept with finches and other small softbills. However, do not attempt to combine them with other birds in a typical small pet cage.

Ringneck Doves

Ringneck Doves *(Streptopelia risoria)* are also referred to as Barbary Doves, but they are mostly known as Ringnecks in the pet trade. These doves are slightly larger than Diamond Doves, measuring approximately 10 inches (25 cm) and weighing about 3 ounces (87 g). They belong to the same genus as Turtledoves and are sometimes incorrectly referred to as such. The normal coloration is beige or pinkish tan with a black band around the back of the neck. However, more than 40 recognized color mutations are available, including white, apricot, and pied. Domestic Ringneck Doves are descended from wild doves of North Africa and have been domesticated and kept as pets far back into history.

Ringneck Doves are sweet and easy to tame, and they can be kept singly if they are given plenty of attention and love. Because they are so popular as pets, they are relatively easy to find in pet shops and at bird fairs. Although they do not require an especially large cage, they will be happiest if they are allowed some free flying time outside of the cage. Never allow them to fly outdoors, however, because they do not have the homing instincts that some pigeons possess, and they will not be able to find their way home.

Enjoying Your Pet

Once you own a dove, you will probably be smitten by these gentle creatures. Research has shown numerous benefits from pet ownership, so living with a dove might even improve your outlook on life! Consider the following:

✔ In study after study, interaction with a pet lowered the participant's blood pressure, heart rate, and cholesterol. Even viewing fish in an aquarium had this effect. Doves, with their soft cooing and calm demeanor, are the perfect antidotes to a stressful day.

✔ Studies have shown that patients who owned pets were less depressed and more involved in their own care. The need to get out of bed and care for a helpless creature is a strong motivator that helps give a depressed or ill person a reason to go on each day.

✔ Pets offer unconditional love and acceptance. Your dove doesn't care if you are rich, successful, or attractive—it will love you just the way you are. Pets ask for little in return: just some fresh food and water, clean accommodations, and a little affection and interaction.

✔ Owning a pet teaches children responsibility. The love and attention they receive in return from the pet can enhance children's self esteem. Doves are excellent pet birds for homes with children.

✔ Pets provide companionship and can lessen loneliness in the elderly or homebound. Studies have shown that elderly people who have pets to care for are more active, less depressed, and less likely to show symptoms of dementia than those without pets. The relatively low-maintenance dove is a wonderful choice for someone who does not have the ability or space to keep a dog or cat.

Please note that not all doves will return your affection in the same manner. Some birds are outgoing and friendly, and others are shy and slightly aloof. Much will depend on the dove's early upbringing, its past experiences with humans, and the amount of time you have to interact and gain its trust on a daily basis. Even an aloof dove, however, will probably crave and enjoy your company in its own way.

In general, tame Ringneck Doves are more likely to enjoy handling and petting. Diamond Doves by nature are a little more flighty, and might be less comfortable being held, but they will enjoy being spoken to gently, being offered treats, and simply going about their daily routine in the company of their human friends. Remember, never place your dove's cage in a remote area of the house or your pet will suffer greatly from loneliness. If you cannot embrace your new pet as a member of the family and give it the love and attention it deserves, then please reconsider your reason for owning a pet.

Because doves make such wonderful pets, it is doubtful you will ever want to give them up. As a matter of fact, more likely you will want to purchase several others to add to your flock! Before you do so, please consider the amount of time needed to care for a single bird and give it the attention it deserves. Start with just one or two birds. As your experience and comfort levels begin to grow, you can add more as space, time, and money permit.

CHOOSING YOUR PET DOVE

Once you have made the decision to add a pet dove to your household, you will want to choose your new companion carefully. A pet dove can live 10–20 years or more with proper care, so this is not a commitment to be taken lightly.

A bird that is sick, extremely fearful, or in poor condition can cost a lot in both time and money. It is ironic, but "bargain" birds usually end up being the most costly choice.

What to Expect

Although doves are relatively inexpensive and low maintenance, especially when compared with other pet birds such as parrots, you should never purchase one on a whim. They are still living creatures that require regular care and attention. You must be able to provide that care consistently, which means daily

It is easy to see how Diamond Doves acquired their name. The beautiful speckling on their feathers makes them look as if they were sprinkled with diamond dust.

feeding and cleaning and veterinary care as needed. Ask yourself the following questions before you proceed:

✔ Have I done research on doves and their pet potential, and am I sure this is a suitable pet for my family and me?

✔ Do I have other animals that might endanger a dove? If so, can I provide safety and security for my new pet? Do I have other birds in the house so that disease transmission might be a factor?

✔ Am I willing to make the commitment of time and money to provide a happy and healthy home for a pet dove? This includes the expense of veterinary care if required.

✔ Do I have small children that might accidentally frighten or injure a bird?

✔ Do I have the space in my home for a suitably sized cage?

What to Do First

Now is the time to familiarize yourself with what you will need to do and what you will need to purchase before you bring your new pet home. Doves are relatively low maintenance, but there are still some basic supplies you will want to have on hand. It will be less stressful for both you and your dove if you are prepared in advance of its arrival.

✔ Will I have time to spend interacting with my pet, or will it be relegated to a back bedroom when my family or I become bored with it?

✔ If I am forced to give up the dove for any reason, am I willing to invest the time and energy to find it a good home? Releasing a tame bird into the wild is a death sentence for the bird and is illegal to boot.

If you have any hesitation after answering these questions, then perhaps you should reconsider your choice of a pet. If, however, you are ready to welcome a pet dove into your life, the next step is finding the right bird.

Where to Begin

Congratulations! You are taking an important first step by reading this book. Now is also the time to decide what species of dove you want and to think about other factors, such as color or gender, that might play into your decision. In general, there is very little difference in the pet potential between male and female doves. Many people prefer to buy doves in pairs so that the birds have companionship of their own kind. This is fine. Keep in mind, though, that visually determining the sex of young birds is difficult, if not impossible. Therefore you will not necessarily know the gender of the birds you are putting together. Some folks claim to be able to tell the difference based on clues like head size and shape—females often have smaller, rounder heads, and are more petite than males. However, these are only educated guesses, and will not necessarily be correct.

Determining gender: The only sure way to determine the sex of an immature bird is to submit a blood sample for DNA analysis or to have your veterinarian examine the bird endoscopically. DNA sexing is simple and noninvasive, using a drop of blood obtained from a clipped toenail or emerging blood feather. Most bird breeders and some pet stores can have this analysis done for you, or you can have your veterinarian perform the test. If you want to get a male and female pair for breeding at a later date, you will need to figure out exactly what you are getting. Of course, none of this is necessary if you are simply looking for a single pet bird.

Nonbreeding companion: If you do prefer to have a companion for your pet but do not want them to breed, your best bet is a same-sex member of the same species. Although mature birds become territorial and might fight with a newcomer of the same gender, two young birds placed together will usually bond easily. Older same-sex birds can also get along well if they are introduced slowly and given plenty of neutral space in the beginning. Although exceptions occur, your pet will likely be unhappy or even in danger if placed with other species. Larger birds, especially parrots, can injure or kill the relatively defenseless dove. Even smaller birds such as finches and canaries might harass and upset your dove in territorial disputes. A stressed, unhappy bird will not be a very good pet and will be prone to all sorts of health problems due to chronic stress.

Where to Find Doves

Once you know what you want, the search begins! There are many sources for pet birds, and it can be confusing. Pet shops, breeders and fanciers, the Internet, bird clubs, and newspapers are just a few places to consider.

Pet Shops

Pet shops are perhaps the easiest place to begin your search. You simply walk in, look at their selection, and make your choice. The downside of pet stores is that they might not have a very wide selection of pet birds, especially doves. If you do see a bird you like, you should consider a few things before making your decision:

✔ Is the store clean? Are the cages clean, properly sized, and well equipped?

✔ Are the birds crowded together or allowed plenty of space to move about?

✔ Are the food and water dishes clean and full? Is the food appropriate for the bird?

✔ Do the birds look healthy and alert or lethargic and scruffy?

✔ Are the store personnel helpful and informed? Can they answer any questions you have?

✔ Does the store have a veterinarian it uses regularly and can recommend?

✔ What kind of health guarantee or return policy does it have?

Pet stores, like any other business, run the gamut from professionally run establishments with healthy animals and knowledgeable staff to dirty storehouses of diseased and poorly kept animals. If you have any doubts, walk out! Buying a pet in order to "rescue" it from a bad environment is always tempting, but this can be an expensive and heartbreaking endeavor. If the shop is truly awful, report it to local authorities, but do not buy from it. Do keep in mind that birds are messy creatures, however, so even the best pet shop in town might sometimes have cages that look unkempt or have water dishes that badly need cleaning. The difference is that a good shop will attend to these problems quickly and show an obvious concern for the welfare of the animals in its care.

Breeders

The advantages of buying straight from breeders is that they will most likely be very

A dove that sits with its feathers fluffed might just be sleepy—or might be sick. Observe the bird carefully.

knowledgeable about the birds they have and they will be able to offer lots of support and advice to new bird owners. The main disadvantage is that they might not be easy to find or conveniently located to where you live. Check newspaper listings under "birds for sale" to find those in your area. You can also ask your veterinarian for information on local bird clubs or fancier associations. Do not be discouraged if local clubs cater more to canary, finch, or parrot owners—these folks might still be able to steer you toward a network of dove enthusiasts.

Another source is Internet dove sites and chat rooms. As mentioned earlier, avoid buying birds from a distance that would require shipping, but do use the Internet to find local breeders or those within a reasonable driving distance.

When buying from a breeder, you should use most of the same checkpoints described for pet shops. There are, however, some major differences. It is unlikely that the person will allow you into the area where the actual breeding birds are kept due to concerns about

A healthy bird stands sleek and alert, with clear eyes and shiny, well-groomed feathers.

security and disease transmission. A parade of strangers in the aviary would frighten and stress the adult birds, which might cause them to desert their nests or injure the babies. Do not think it suspicious or odd if the breeder refuses you access to these areas. Instead, take a look at where and how the chicks are being kept. They should be in clean and spacious cages, be alert and calm. Ideally they should be willing to tolerate some handling. If a bird is a little nervous or shy, that is okay. However, avoid any that are frantic and fearful around people.

Bird Fairs

One sure harbinger of spring in many areas of the country is the appearance of bird fairs. These large gatherings of breeders, enthusiasts, and merchants offer a wide array of pet birds and bird products. You can find listings for upcoming fairs in local newspapers or in avicultural magazines such as *Bird Talk*. Like pet shops, the fairs usually focus mostly on canaries, finches, and parrots, but doves are often available. You might also find game bird shows in your area, which will usually include pigeon and dove breeders.

If you decide to buy a bird at a bird fair, do not be afraid to ask a lot of questions of the seller. Most importantly, be certain to get the person's name, address, and phone number in case you need to contact him or her with questions about the bird's health and background. Although many experienced and reputable breeders exhibit at fairs, unfortunately some less-reputable types knowingly bring sick or poor-quality birds to dump. Most fairs are run by clubs, which do their best to police the vendors. However, anticipating shady dealers is not always possible. Feel free to ask the seller about any club affiliations or references he or she might have. Breeders often swap and sell birds to each other, so you may be able to check references without even leaving the exhibit hall.

Bringing Your Bird Home

Once you have chosen your new dove, the time has come to bring it home. If you have done your research in advance, you should already have the cage, food, and all necessary supplies at home. If you are not set up and ready to go, you should probably hold off on purchasing the bird or ask the breeder if you can make arrangements to pick it up at a later date. Going to a new home is stressful for a bird. Your dove will experience even more stress if it has to spend hours closed up in a box on the floor while you rush around trying to set up its accommodations. Please do the preparations in advance, and you will find the transition more pleasant for both you and your new pet!

Quarantine

If you already have other pet birds of any species, you must quarantine your new dove for approximately 30 days. This is crucial for the safety of both the existing birds and your new addition. Birds hide illness very well. Even if the dove you have selected appears perfectly healthy, it could be carrying pathogens that are deadly to the birds you already own. On the other hand, your old pets might be asymptomatic carriers of a disease that does not make them sick but can kill a newcomer.

True quarantine is a complicated process that takes into consideration such things as airflow patterns and air filtration. Creating a foolproof quarantine in a regular home is pretty much impossible. However, you can do several things to reduce the chances of disease transmission.

✔ Temporarily keep your new pet in a room separate from existing birds, such as a spare bedroom or home office.

✔ Always wash your hands thoroughly after handling any birds or servicing cages before you move on to the next bird.

✔ If you have been holding or playing with your pets, shower and change clothes before you move on to the newcomer or vice versa.

✔ Do not intermingle food.

✔ Keep a separate sponge and cleaning utensils for each cage.

✔ Use a different broom to sweep each room that houses birds.

✔ Keep a separate set of dishes for each cage, and disinfect them carefully after use.

✔ Restrict other pets, such as cats and dogs, from entering the quarantine room, because they can track germs from one area to the next.

Although this might sound like a lot of trouble, it is important to do as much as possible to protect your pets. After about 30 days, you can start to relax the above procedures and move your dove into the same room with your other birds if you desire. You should still wash your hands between handling different birds. If they are all healthy, though, you should not have much to worry about. As mentioned earlier, this is not a strict quarantine, and some diseases can remain hidden for months if not years. However, these commonsense precautions will

TIP

Clean Hands

Keep a bottle of waterless hand sanitizer gel near your cages, and get in the habit of using it before and after handling your birds and their accessories. Even if your dove is the only bird in the household, your hands can still transmit dangerous germs to your pet, so keep them clean!

go a long way in ensuring the health of your flock. Of course, if you do not have other pet birds, then quarantine is not necessary. It is still important, however, to observe your dove carefully for the first few weeks to watch for possible signs of illness.

The First Few Days

Your dove will most likely be a little frightened and disoriented in its new home. Keep the area around its cage quiet, and keep children and other pets from harassing the newcomer. Move slowly and speak quietly until your dove begins to recognize and accept you. Give your pet plenty of sleep time—at least 10 hours a night—in a darkened environment. If the cage is in a family room or other spot where this might be difficult, a good cage cover will darken the cage and block out some of the family noise. Give the bird time to observe you in a nonthreatening situation. For example, spend some time reading or watching television (quietly) near your dove's cage. It will soon grow accustomed to your presence and begin to welcome your companionship.

Spend time talking with the seller and learn all you can about the type of dove you plan to buy.

Although it is tempting to buy a dove based on its beauty, be certain that you can provide properly for its care.

Give your new pet some quiet time to settle in once you bring it home. After all, moving is stressful!

The first step in determining a dove's health is to observe it from a distance. Birds are prey animals, which means that they will do everything in their power to hide illness or injury lest they become a target for a predator looking for a quick lunch. If a dove knows you are watching it, it will attempt to appear normal and healthy. Instead, find a spot where you can see the bird but it cannot easily see you. Watch carefully, and be aware of the following points.

Posture and Movement

A healthy bird will appear alert and will move about easily. Avoid a bird that appears lethargic, lame, or reluctant to move. A sleepy bird might tuck its head under its feathers for a short nap. However, a bird that buries its head in its feathers for an extended period during the day, or seems slow to rouse, might very well be sick.

Feathers

A healthy bird has feathers that are smooth, bright, and held closely to the body. A dove with feathers that are dull, fluffed, or missing in patches is probably not healthy. Birds will commonly fluff their feathers when cold or sleepy, but a healthy bird will tighten its feathers as soon as it wakes from its nap or begins to move about. Missing feathers can be simply a result of being picked on by cagemates, but it can also signify disease or parasites.

Eyes

Both eyes should be bright, alert, and free of discharge or swellings. A dove with dull, listless eyes is likely very sick.

Signs of Discomfort

A bird that constantly rubs its face on a perch, or that pumps its tail up and down as it breathes, is probably suffering from a respiratory disease. Other respiratory warning signs include open-mouthed breathing, nasal or ocular discharge, frequent head shaking, sneezing, or a clicking sound as the bird breathes.

Other signs of discomfort, such as picking at feathers, frequent scratching and poking at the skin, or frantic pacing interspersed with scratching, might indicate parasites. Do not confuse these signs with normal preening and grooming, which a healthy bird will do in a relaxed manner before it moves on to other activities.

Hands-on Health Check

Now that you have observed from a distance, it is time to move in for a hands-on health check. Gently pick up the dove. Take a closer look at its eyes, nostrils, and beak, which should all be clean and free of discharge or injury. The legs, feet, and toes

A sick dove will appear lethargic, fluffed, and weak. Steer clear, or you risk high veterinary bills, possible heartbreak, and the risk of infecting other birds in your home.

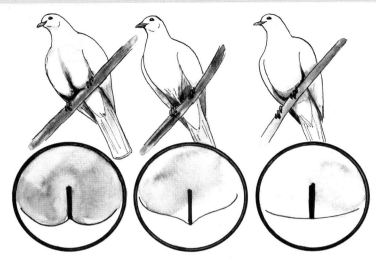

A bird's weight is a good indicator of its overall health. An overweight bird will have cleavage on either side of its breastbone (keel). A sick bird might appear thin, with a prominent keel and sunken chest. A healthy bird will have a smooth, well-rounded chest area with a keel bone that is barely visible.

should be well scaled but smooth and free of any sores or inflamed areas.

Next, check the bird's weight. The easiest way to do this is to examine the keel bone, which is the breastbone that runs down the center of a bird's chest. On an overweight dove, you will barely be able to feel the bone. If a bird is underweight, the bone will feel prominent, almost sharp. Never buy an underweight bird, because weight loss is one of the first signs of disease.

Lift the dove up to observe its vent area, which should be clean and free of debris. If the bird's vent feathers are wet or pasted with dried feces, the dove might have gastrointestinal disease or parasites.

The Dove's Reaction

Consider how the dove has reacted to your handling. If it has remained calm and alert (but not lethargic or listless) and if it appears healthy based on the points described previously, you have probably found a great pet. If it appears healthy but is nervous and slightly reluctant to be held, it can still be a good pet if you are willing to invest some time to earn its trust.

Avoid a bird that is frantic and terrified of handling, even if it appears healthy. Some birds just do not have the personality or desire for human companionship.

Of course, if a bird displays any of the signs of illness listed above, do not purchase it with the hope that it will get better under your care.

Although that is certainly possible, an already ill bird faced with the stress of moving to a new home has an awful lot going against it. Point out your concerns to the pet shop owner or breeder, and look elsewhere to find a healthy pet that will be around to share your life for a long time.

UNDERSTANDING YOUR DOVE

Probably the most important aspect of bonding with your new pet is learning to interpret and understand its behavior. People often give advice about how to "tame" a bird as if this were simply another trick to be taught. In reality, true tameness comes from a mutual give and take of affection and respect and really needs to be earned rather than enforced.

Once you understand what your dove is communicating to you through its behavior, you will learn to respond in a manner that convinces the bird that you are a trusted friend and not a threat to its safety.

The Dove's World

You must remember two things about doves: They are flock animals and they are prey animals. These two factors influence everything about how they relate to the world around them.

White-winged Doves are native to Central America and the southern United States, as well as parts of South America.

As flock animals, they are social and crave companionship. This does not necessarily mean that doves cannot be kept singly. Just be aware that a tame pet will be happiest if it has daily interaction with you. A bird that is caged alone and then largely ignored will most likely suffer from boredom and loneliness. Understand before you purchase a bird that you must be willing to satisfy its emotional needs in addition to purely physical needs such as food and water. Although doves are not quite as emotionally needy as some other birds (parrots, for example), they still are not a low-maintenance pet.

On the other hand, their stature as prey animals means they need to view their surroundings with a great deal of caution and suspicion.

When you are relatively low down on the food chain, trust is not an emotion that comes easily. To survive, they always must be on the lookout for that circling hawk or stalking feline, or risk being something's next meal.

From that perspective, a ceiling fan looks an awful lot like the onrushing wings of a hawk or falcon. Any creature (including a well-meaning human) that stares intensely without looking away appears to be on the hunt. A smiling human (all those teeth!) that stares might even be more frightening. This does not mean you cannot ever stare or smile at your pet. However, you might understand dove behavior a little better if you occasionally look at the world through your bird's eyes. Once your pet becomes accustomed to your actions and learns that you do not intend any harm, it will become much more tolerant of your movements and body language.

Dove Behavior

Once you and your bird are comfortable with each other, you will probably start to wonder how to interpret your pet's different behaviors. Some of its body language might be obvious—it is pretty easy to guess that a frantically thrashing bird is probably frightened. However, other actions are much more subtle and might appear puzzling. The following discusses a few of the most common behaviors and what they mean.

Fear: A fearful dove will stand very tall, hold its wings tightly against its body, flatten its feathers, and freeze in place. Predators are attracted to movement, so a "frozen" dove is much less likely to be seen in the wild. Your pet might do this if it hears a loud or unfamiliar noise or if it sees something that appears threatening, such as a cat, dog, or human stranger. If the perceived danger moves closer and the dove knows it has been spotted, it will usually try to fly away. A panicked bird will fly rapidly and blindly and can injure itself by flying into walls, ceilings, or cage bars.

Contentment: A relaxed bird will move about in a casual manner, show interest in its surroundings without fixating on any one thing, and likely spend a great deal of time preening its feathers. Feathers are vital to a bird's life; they provide insulation, help regulate body temperature, and through flight allow a bird to escape from predators. You will often see your pet running its beak through its feathers to clean and straighten them. Mated pairs of doves will preen each other in a display of affection and bonding.

A relaxed dove will also periodically fluff and shake out its feathers, especially after preening or after a nap. Birds do this in part to remove debris and dust, but it also seems to be a calming ritual. Feather fluffing is often accompanied by stretching of the wings and body, just as humans stretch and yawn after a tedious task.

Anger: Doves are not usually too prone to displays of anger, but they can be territorial when defending their nest, squabs, or mate. An angry dove will stand its ground, fan out its tail feathers, and sometimes lift one or both wings to make itself look larger and more threatening. It might ruffle up some feathers around its head or rump in the same manner as angry dogs or cats will raise the fur on their necks. Some doves will jab rapidly with their beaks in the direction of the intruder. When sparring with another bird, doves will often use their wings to slap at the offender or will slap their wing on the ground in warning.

Dove courtship: Rituals can be very intricate and very vocal. In general, the male begins the ritual by cooing to let interested females know he is available. When he spots a female he wants, he will then puff up his chest and repeatedly bow down in front of her while cooing. In some species, the male will also nod his head or peck himself repeatedly behind the wings. If the female is suitably impressed by his display, she might nod or coo in return, or she will droop her wings and fan her tail to let the male know she is interested. Sometimes the pair will rub beaks, and the male might open his beak to offer regurgitated food to the hen. A male will also droop and flutter his wings, especially when he is showing off a suitable nesting site.

Illness: Distinguishing between normal and unnatural behavior in your pet is very important because unusual actions can signify illness. As prey animals, they must keep up with the flock and hide signs of sickness for as long as possible, because a predator seeks out the weakest or slowest members of a group. That means that your pet might not show obvious signs of illness until it is near death and too weak to maintain the facade anymore. Signs of a sick bird include lack of appetite, glassy or dull eyes, ruffled or unkempt feathers, and foul-smelling or loose droppings. This will be discussed in more detail in the chapter on health care, but be aware that behavioral changes can signify illness in your pet.

Establishing Trust

Before you buy your pet, you should spend some time observing the bird and watch how it

Behavior—Yours and Your Dove's

The discussion of behaviors under "Establishing Trust" is by no means all-inclusive, but it will give you a good start at understanding what your dove's actions mean. Once you develop a bond with your pet and spend some time observing it on a daily basis, you will soon know what is normal and what is not. At the same time, your bird will be observing you. It will learn to understand what your actions mean, in much the same way that the family cat comes running when it hears a can opener!

interacts with the seller. Avoid doves that seem very frightened or panicked, because they will be more difficult for a beginner to tame. A good dove breeder will spend time with his or her birds and make sure they are properly socialized. If you purchase a young dove that was handled from an early age, it might already be comfortable with humans and easy to handle. In any case, some gentle "get acquainted" sessions will help you to establish a bond with your new pet.

Where to Bond

Begin by finding a quiet, safe place in your home for the taming process. Do not attempt these sessions in a busy room or in any place where family members or other pets might be a distraction or danger. A bathroom or other small room where you can close the door is ideal. Make certain to remove any possible hazards, should your bird become frightened and take flight. For example, close toilet lids, turn off ceiling fans, and shut windows.

Doves are relatively inexpensive compared to many other cage bird species.

Although there are over 300 species in the dove and pigeon family, only a few are suitable as indoor pets.

Diamond Doves have a gentle disposition and do well as single pets or in pairs.

The Crested pigeon requires plenty of room to fly and does best in warm and dry conditions.

Clipped Wings

If your new pet is very skittish, you might want to have its wings clipped before you begin. This is a painless and temporary way of limiting a bird's flight capabilities, akin to a haircut in humans. The clipped feathers will eventually molt out and be replaced, and your bird will once again be able to fly normally. A clipped bird is much easier to tame and will be less likely to injure itself if it becomes frightened or startled.

The Approach

Once you are ready, slowly approach your bird from the front and gently pick it up by cupping your hands around its body. Do not grab it from behind or above, because that is how a predator would attack. You can set it on your lap or place your index finger under its feet so that it is perching on your hand. If it flutters away, repeat the process while talking softly and moving slowly.

It is fine to make eye contact, but glance away frequently or blink your eyes in a slow, exaggerated manner so your bird does not feel threatened by your gaze.

Offer the bird a favored treat from your hand. A wiggling mealworm works great or a small piece of millet spray. If the bird seems pretty calm and willing to perch on you, then you can spend as much time as you like enjoying each other's company. If it is obviously frightened and stressed, end the session after a few minutes and try again later. With patience, even a nervous dove should eventually calm enough to tolerate some handling. In general, doves are not cuddly birds like some parrots, but most will enjoy spending time with humans they trust.

Be Patient

Keep in mind that to earn your pet's trust, you must be patient and consistent. Never attempt a taming session if you are feeling angry, frustrated, or somehow out of sorts. Birds are incredibly sensitive and will likely pick up your moods and respond accordingly. Also be aware of how others in your household interact with the bird. All your hard work at building a relationship might be lost if someone else is harassing or otherwise mistreating your pet when you are not around. With birds, you very much reap what you sow. If you treat your pet with kindness and affection, you will likely get the same in return.

Children

Although most children love animals, they need to be taught how to interact properly with the pet, and an adult should supervise those interactions, at least in the beginning. Doves make great pets for kids, provided the child is able to follow a few basic rules of conduct. A dove will not appreciate being grabbed roughly, chased, or teased. Teach your children to handle the bird gently, and to keep their movements slow and quiet. They need to understand that a bird will be very frightened by the same rough-and-tumble play that might delight the family dog. If the child is not old enough to handle the bird properly, then limit interaction until the child is a little older. With some time and coaching from mom or dad, they will likely be best friends in a short time.

Other Pets

If you have other pets in your household, including other species of birds, do not expect them to become friends with your dove. Dogs, cats, snakes, and ferrets are natural predators, and your dove is unlikely to ever consider them anything but a threat. In time, your dove will learn to accept the presence of other animals in the household without becoming panicked, *provided* you have instilled a sense of safety and security in its life. Keep the dove's cage at a safe height well out of reach of curious paws and probing snouts. Never let your bird out of its cage unless other pets are securely contained in another room. It would take only one moment of distraction for your dove to be attacked and killed by another pet. A dove that is in constant fear for its life is unlikely to act in a relaxed and tame manner.

The same holds true for mixing doves with other species of birds. Because parrots aren't predators and are unlikely to stalk a dove, you can allow different birds out of the cage in the same room at the same time, but always supervise to ensure that they do not get too close to each other. Your dove might not have an instinctive fear of another bird and might venture into the parrot's territory (for example, landing on the parrot's cage) causing an aggressive reaction. Parrots have very strong beaks and claws, and could easily kill or severely injure the relatively defenseless dove. Even a very small member of the parrot family, such as

a budgie or cockatiel, will have a beak strength and agility that your dove cannot match.

Other Doves

As mentioned earlier, doves do very well when kept in pairs, provided the cage is large enough to accommodate two birds. If you do keep a pair of doves, be aware that the birds will likely respond to you in a different manner than a bird kept singly. When you keep a single bird, you are the center of its universe and the one that it will look to for companionship and affection. When you keep two doves together, the birds become bonded to each other, and might be less inclined to desire quite as much interaction with humans.

This does not mean that they won't be good pets, or that they can be stuffed away in a remote corner of the home, but the dynamics of the relationship are different. The birds will still want to be around humans, but they will spend much of their time interacting with each other. This can be a joy to watch, and is a good solution for folks who want a dove but who work long hours and worry about the amount of quality time they can provide. Again, buying two doves does not give you license to ignore them, but it will keep your pets from becoming lonely during those stretches of time when no one is home.

Before you bring your dove home, you will have to set up a suitable cage. The type of cage you choose is important for both you and your dove. A poorly made, hard to clean cage will drive you crazy every time you attempt to clean it and make cleaning chores much more difficult than they ought to be.

Your dove will not be happy in a cage that is too small, badly designed, or the wrong shape. Spend some time looking at various cages, and buy the biggest and the best you can afford. Your pet will appreciate the room, and you will appreciate the quality.

Indoor Cages

Because the topic of this book is small pet doves, we will focus mostly on indoor cages. Larger doves and pigeons require much more space and room to fly. They need to be housed in large outdoor aviaries or flight cages.

Cage Size

A single pet or a pair of Ringneck or Diamond

Never buy a species that requires more space or care than you can provide. Ultimately, the bird will suffer from your decision.

Doves can be housed comfortably in a large cockatiel-sized cage, but remember, the larger the better. Your pet needs room to flap its wings and exercise, so look for a cage at least 24 inches (60 cm) in length, preferably 36 inches (90 cm). Doves do not climb like parrots, so length is much more important than height. The cage should be no less than 16 inches (40 cm) wide and at least 18–24 inches (45–60 cm) tall. Even with these minimum sizes, your pet will probably be happiest if it is allowed some supervised flight time out of the cage.

Bars

Because doves do not have the same beak strength as parrots, the wire gauge of the cage is not important—your pet will not be able to bend or break even thin bars. The bar spacing, however, is important. The bars should be set closely enough together so that your pet cannot stick its head through them and get

Cage Checkpoints

✔ Is the cage a suitable size and shape for my pet? Is it large enough to accommodate a second dove if I decide to add another?

✔ Is it made of quality materials? Is the bar spacing appropriate?

✔ Does it have a pull-out tray to provide easy access for cleaning?

✔ How does the door operate? Doors that open from the top and hinge forward (known as landing-style doors) make it easier for your pet to return to its cage after free flight time. Avoid guillotine-style doors that lift up and drop down. These can pose a danger to birds if they are able to lift the door, because it can fall back down and trap feet or heads.

✔ Does it have sufficient room for food and water dishes, perches, and a scratching pan without crowding my pet?

✔ Are there any sharp edges or gaps that might pose a danger?

caught. The smaller Diamond Doves will be safer in a cage designed for budgies or finches, provided it is sufficiently large.

Buy or Make?

You can find a wide variety of cages at pet shops, feed stores, and on the Internet. If you are handy, you can also make your own cage out of galvanized wire. Some doves, especially breeding pairs that like the feeling of security, do well in box cages. These are cages made from plywood with wire just on the front. The disadvantage to these is that they offer poor ventilation and are difficult to clean and disinfect.

Safety Issues

Whatever type of cage you choose, look for safety features and ease of cleaning. Avoid cages with sharp edges, large gaps a bird could get its foot or head stuck in, and cages made of questionable materials. For example, antique and decorative cages might have unacceptable levels of lead, zinc, or other toxic heavy metals. Avoid cheaply painted or plastic-coated bars that might flake or peel.

If you buy used cages, keep in mind that the previous occupant might have died from an infectious disease or been overwhelmed by parasites, and these dangers might still be lurking in crevices, waiting to attack your bird. Always scrub and disinfect a used cage thoroughly. The money saved does not justify the risk. Your best bet is to buy a new cage designed for pet birds from a reputable dealer. The breeder or store from which you purchase your dove can probably give you some good recommendations.

Cage Placement

Once you have decided on a suitable cage, the next step is to decide where to place the cage in your home. Your pet will want to be in a spot where it is able to interact with the family, but it will also want to feel safe and secure. Please do not buy a single bird and stick it in a back bedroom or other place where it is left alone and largely ignored. Doves are loving and affectionate creatures, and they will suffer greatly without the companionship of either a mate or a human friend. The ideal spot would be a protected corner of a family room or other place you spend some time relaxing. Place the cage high enough to keep it out of reach of other pets. Birds feel most secure when they're up high, so never place the cage on the floor or a low stand.

You should also be aware of drafts. Although doves are hardy birds, your pet will not be comfortable if it is placed near a drafty window in winter or an air-conditioning vent in summer. On the other hand, do not place the cage next to a heating vent or in front of a window where it will be in direct sunlight, or your bird might overheat. In general, your dove will be comfortable in the same temperature range that you are, so place the cage accordingly.

Lighting

Because your dove is living indoors, it will not have ready access to healthy sunlight. Sunlight, or full-spectrum artificial lighting, is required by your bird to manufacture vitamin D_3. Vitamin D_3 acts as a hormone in the body and is necessary for proper utilization of calcium. Birds deficient in this vitamin might exhibit poor bone growth, easily broken or deformed bones, seizures, and egg-laying problems.

Full-spectrum lightbulbs: Because window glass blocks many of the beneficial ultraviolet rays, placing your pet near a window will not help much. Instead, you can purchase full-spectrum lightbulbs from pet shops, hardware stores, or on the Internet. Place this lighting near your bird's cage. These bulbs come in both fluorescent and incandescent versions, in many shapes and sizes. Look for the words "full-spectrum" or "provides beneficial UV" or words to that effect. Some popular brand names are Vitalite, Ott lights, and Verilux, but dozens of others are available. These lights mimic the range of rays produced by the Sun and will help keep your indoor bird healthy.

Sun bath: You can also give your pet an occasional Sun bath by bringing its cage out onto your patio or deck for a few hours during nice weather. If you do this, you must keep a few safety points in mind. Never bring your bird out during the hottest times of the day. Never leave it in direct sunlight, or it will overheat. Make sure at least part of the cage is shaded so the dove can move to a cooler area. Keep the cage off the ground and safe from predators, such as the neighbor's cat or hungry birds of prey. Provide plenty of fresh water, and offer a shallow dish for bathing so your bird can cool off. Do not leave your bird unattended outdoors. Keep in mind that an indoor pet cage does not offer the same protection from predators that a permanent outdoor flight cage would, so bring the bird back indoors if you cannot supervise.

Air Quality

Indoor air quality is important for both your bird's health and your own. Most birds, including doves, give off a fine powdery feather dust that can aggravate allergies in susceptible people. In addition, molds, bacteria, pollen, viruses, and other airborne toxins can all accumulate in the air inside the typical home, making the air we breathe less than healthy. Simply opening windows whenever possible will do a lot to freshen the air and allow toxins to escape.

To improve your air quality, though, you will need an air purifier. Although an air purifier is not a strict necessity, both you and your pet will breathe easier with one. The best air purifiers offer HEPA quality filtration. This means that they are capable of removing most airborne pollutants, including microscopic particles. Choose one that is properly rated for the

Above all, doves need a variety of perches to keep their feet in good condition.

size of the room you will use it in, and make sure that replacement filters are readily available and affordable. Some air purifiers also generate negative ions, which give the air the same fresh feeling as after a thunderstorm. However, these can also produce ozone, which can be harmful and cause breathing difficulties.

Cage Accessories

Now that you have attended to the cage and its surroundings, it is time to set up the cage interior. Doves, unlike parrots, do not play with or require toys. They will need a variety of good perching surfaces, some sturdy food and water dishes, and perhaps a scratching pan filled with sand and a shallow dish for bathing.

Food and water dishes: A wide variety of feeders and dishes are available at most pet shops. Doves are not particularly fussy about which type they use, but you will want to purchase those that are sturdy and easy to clean. Always position the cups away from perching surfaces so that they are not fouled by droppings. Covered dishes have the advantage that

Unlike many other cage birds, doves do not play with toys. Your pet might, however, appreciate a shallow pan of grit or clean sand to scratch around in.

the birds cannot defecate into them as easily, but still place them safely away from perches. Dishes should be placed at or below perch level.

You will need one dish for water, one for seed, and a third for any fresh foods you offer. Once you find dishes you like, I suggest buying two sets. That way, you can remove the dirty set and toss them into the dishwasher, and you will always have a clean set ready to go. If you do not have a dishwasher, or prefer not to use it, then scrub the dirty dishes thoroughly with hot water and dish soap daily.

Perches: Always offer your pet a variety of different perching surfaces to help keep its feet comfortable and well exercised. The plain wooden dowel perches sold with most birdcages are not really a very good choice. Because of their uniform diameter and smooth surface, your bird runs the risk of developing pressure sores on its feet from standing on the same surface all the time. Many manufacturers now offer natural wood branches with varying thicknesses and textures. You can also cut branches from trees and use them as perches. However, always scrub and disinfect them with a mild solution of bleach and water, and then rinse and dry thoroughly before you put them into your pet's cage. Your dove will also enjoy a flat perch or ledge to walk around on. However, use common sense and do not crowd the cage so that your pet cannot flap its wings and move about freely.

Baths: Doves love to bathe, so you can place a shallow pan on the cage floor with a little water in it. Do not leave the pan in the cage to be fouled with food and droppings, but offer it a few times a week or daily in hot weather. Make sure the water is lukewarm, and no more than about ½ inch (1 cm) or so deep. The container must be very shallow. A pie tin or plant saucer works well. Never use a tall container or deeper water, because your pet could drown.

Some birds will also bathe by rolling around in wet greens. You can place a large handful of very wet spinach or lettuce leaves on a plate in the cage. Your bird can bathe and then nibble on the greens for a healthy snack.

Scratching pan: Some doves will enjoy scratching around on the bottom of their cage. To keep the mess confined a bit, you can offer a shallow tray or pan filled with clean sand. Replace the sand every few days as it becomes soiled.

Cage covers: Covering your pet's cage at night is optional. If you are the early to bed type, chances are your bird will get enough rest. If you are a family of night owls, however, a sturdy, dark fabric cover will allow your dove the darkness and privacy to sleep while the rest of the household is active. Cage covers can be purchased at many pet stores, or simply use a dark sheet or other piece of suitable fabric.

Outdoor Aviaries

If you decide to keep more than a single pair of small doves, or you want to keep larger species, you might decide to build an outdoor aviary. Before you proceed, you should consider some questions:

✔ Do the local zoning laws or building ordinances allow you to keep birds outdoors? Some communities have strict laws limiting pet ownership or outdoor cages.

✔ Will you have problems with the neighbors? Although doves are not noisy, nearby neighbors might complain about the cooing or claim your birds attract rodents and create a public health hazard.

Always position food and water dishes safely away from perches. Otherwise, your bird will be prone to perch above and poop in them, fouling the dishes with droppings.

✔ Can you provide proper shelter from inclement weather and predators? That includes heating in cool weather and cooling in extreme heat.

✔ Do you have easy access to water and electricity for cleaning and servicing the aviary?

The structure: Aviaries can be built with either a wooden or concrete block frame. Keep in mind that wood can rot and might attract termites or carpenter ants, so at least the base should be concrete if possible to keep the wood from having contact with the ground. Use galvanized wire or hardware cloth to cover the frame, and bury the wire at least 12 inches (30 cm) into the ground to prevent predators from digging their way in. New wire should always be scrubbed thoroughly with a 1:1 solution of water and white vinegar to remove traces of manufacturing chemicals, zinc, or other metal residues. The floor of the aviary can be concrete, which is easiest to clean, or sand, gravel, or earth. Whichever you choose,

When keeping doves in outdoor aviaries, be sure you provide plenty of protection from the elements and from predators.

make sure to clean it frequently by raking away debris and hosing it down.

Size: Aviary size depends on the number and species of doves you wish to keep, but always allow plenty of space. Overcrowded doves will likely fight and become stressed. In general, a flight cage for four pairs of small doves should measure approximately 8 feet (240 cm) long by 4 feet (120 cm) wide by 6 feet (180 cm) tall. Medium-sized species would require even larger accommodations.

Comfort considerations: Every outdoor aviary must also have an attached shelter so the birds can escape foul weather. A small wooden shed or similar structure that can be heated and cooled as necessary is ideal. Doves can handle a pretty wide range of temperatures if they are acclimated to it, but extreme heat or cold can be deadly. In northern climates, adding a small portable heater might be necessary during the coldest part of winter. Oil-filled types resemble radiators, and these are relatively safe and do not emit fumes. During hot summer months, you can run a small air-conditioning unit set on low to cool the shelter. At the very least, install some vents or skylights that can be opened for ventilation. Of course, cover any openings with wire so the birds cannot escape.

Escape prevention: To prevent escape, you will also need to devise a double-door system for your aviary. Doves are quick and talented fliers, and they can easily shoot past you as you enter the aviary for feeding or cleaning. Create a small vestibule with its own door that you enter before entering the bird area. That way, if a bird does fly past you, it will simply be trapped in the vestibule. Another safety measure is to drape the entire aviary with mosquito netting. This serves two purposes. If a bird escapes the flight cage, it will be trapped in the netting and unable to escape. The netting also prevents disease-carrying mosquitoes and other insects from having easy access to your doves.

Cleaning and Disinfection

To keep your dove healthy, you will need to keep its cage and utensils clean. Pathogens are everywhere, and they will travel through the air and set up housekeeping wherever they find a suitable spot. Only regular cleaning and disinfection as needed keeps them at bay. You will not be able to keep you dove's cage and utensils sterile, nor should you want to. However, the old adage, "An ounce of prevention is worth a pound of cure," certainly applies. If you properly clean and disinfect your bird's accommodations, you will decrease the chance of it becoming ill.

First, you should understand the difference between cleaning and disinfection. Cleaning is a means of physically removing dirt and germs from a surface, usually with soap and water. If you have a single pet bird or two and they are not sick, cleaning is good enough most of the time. You should clean certain items every day in order to insure your bird's health.

Cleaning Responsibilities

✔ Clean food and water dishes daily. To do so, scrub with hot water and dish soap. If possible, wash the dishes in the dishwasher. While they are in the dishwasher, remember to provide your bird with another set of clean food and water dishes. If your bird soils its water dish with feces, you should clean it—even if you have already done the daily cleaning.

Remember that harmful bacteria can grow rapidly, especially in hot weather. Change the water whenever it appears soiled, but never less frequently than once a day. Your bird will not like drinking dirty water any more than you would.

✔ Clean perches daily. To do so, scrape off all debris and heavy soiling. A few times a week, or as needed, scrub perches in hot, soapy water, rinse, and dry thoroughly.

✔ Clean the cage daily. To clean a cage with a bird inside, scrape off all visible debris and wipe down with a scrubby sponge and plain warm water. For stubborn spots, rub with a paste of baking soda and water. Change cage papers or litter on a daily basis. For a more thorough periodic cleaning, remove the bird from the cage. Place it safely into a pet carrier or have another family member supervise it out of the cage. Small cages can be placed into the sink or bathtub for a thorough cleaning in hot, soapy water. If your cage is too large to fit in the tub, you can bring it outside and hose it off or use a pressure washer to remove more stubborn debris.

Disinfection

Disinfection kills germs on a surface, usually through chemical means or extreme heat. Disinfection is important if you have a sick bird, are introducing new birds to your home, or have an object that might be contaminated. True disinfection is a four-step process.

✔ Step one: The object must be cleaned to remove the dirt and organic debris.

✔ Step two: The object must be rinsed thoroughly.

✔ Step three: The disinfectant must then be applied.

✔ Step four: After allowing the recommended contact time, the object must once again be rinsed completely.

All disinfectants have what is known as a contact time. This is the length of time the product must be in contact with the object in order to destroy germs. In general, the contact time is at least 10 minutes. The container holding the disinfectant will specify the contact time on the label. Simply spraying a disinfectant onto a surface and then immediately wiping it clean might not be any more effective than cleaning with regular soap and water. In fact, this sloppy process can actually leave behind potentially dangerous residue.

Types of Disinfectants

Disinfectants are usually pretty harsh chemicals, so use them carefully. You can purchase many different brands through your veterinarian or on the Internet that are recommended for use around pets. You can also use a solution of ½ cup (120 mL) of bleach mixed with 1 gallon (4 L) of water. Always use with proper ventilation and rinse objects well before returning them to the cage. Chlorine (bleach) fumes are very hazardous to birds and can damage their respiratory system.

Additional Cautions

Remember to read the label carefully before using any disinfecting product. If necessary, wear latex gloves when using the chemical. These can be found in most hardware stores or in the household cleansers section of most supermarkets. You should not breathe in the fumes from any disinfectant and should keep windows open to allow for proper ventilation when using a product. Always keep all chemicals in their original bottles. A final word of caution: Never, ever mix chemicals. Doing so can create hazardous fumes, which can harm or kill your dove or you.

How to Disinfect

The following are some hints for disinfecting your pet's cage and accessories.

✔ Food and water dishes: To disinfect, scrub with hot water and dish soap. If possible, wash in the dishwasher. Then soak in disinfectant for the recommended time. Rinse thoroughly before use.

✔ Perches: Do not soak wooden perches in disinfectant. To disinfect, bake in the oven at a low temperature (200°F [93°C]) for about one-half hour to kill most pathogens. If the wood is very dirty or contaminated, throw it out and replace it.

✔ Cages: To disinfect, spray or wipe all cage surfaces with disinfectant solution. Continue to spray or wipe to keep the solution wet for at least 10 minutes or as directed by the disinfectant's label. Rinse and dry carefully before putting your bird back inside.

Disinfection Schedule

There is no standard schedule for disinfection. Much will depend on the number of birds you keep, and the health of your birds. Please remember that disinfection is performed in addition to regular cleaning, never in place of it! Always use common sense, and disinfect as needed. The following are some general recommendations:

✔ For a single healthy pet bird or a single mated pair, disinfect perches monthly. Food and water dishes do not require routine disinfection if you are washing them daily in the dishwasher or in hot soapy water. If the dishes get cracked or porous, or are otherwise hard to clean properly, it is best to replace them. Disinfect the cage a few times a year (seasonally is a good idea) after you have given it a thorough cleaning.

✔ In multiple (healthy) bird households, disinfect perches weekly. If food and water dishes are switched between cages, then disinfect between use. Cages should be disinfected monthly.

✔ In case of a disease outbreak, you must disinfect all items frequently, and exercise great caution to avoid transmitting pathogens between birds. Ask your veterinarian to recommend the appropriate disinfectant for the suspected pathogen, and use as directed. In general, the cage, perches, and utensils of sick birds and those in the same household should probably be disinfected on a daily basis.

Too Much of a Good Thing

One word of caution: although cleanliness is very important, it can be taken it to the extreme. You do not need to follow your bird around with a spray bottle of cleaner, lunging at every dropping or stray bit of food. A certain low level of pathogens is normal in the environment and actually helps keep the immune system in good working order. Like everything else, let common sense be your guide. Keep the cage and utensils clean, disinfect them periodically, and enjoy your happy and healthy dove.

HEALTHY NUTRITION

One of the most important ways to ensure your pet lives a long and happy life is to feed it a varied and nutritious diet. A good diet needs to be fresh and palatable. It must provide a wide range of nutrients to keep your dove in top health.

Some avian veterinarians have estimated that a majority of pet bird diseases are caused or exacerbated by improper nutrition. A poorly fed bird might have feathers that look dull or rough, suffer from frequent respiratory or gastric ailments, and might experience breeding difficulties such as infertility or egg binding. Even minor deficiencies can cause subtle health changes and can shorten your pet's life span. On the other hand, an overfed bird or one that picks through its dish and chooses only high-fat foods can suffer the same types of obesity-related diseases as humans.

What Is a Healthy Diet?

So what constitutes a healthy diet? To sustain life, a diet must contain several essential

The effects of a good diet are obvious in the sleek, shiny feathers and bright eyes of this healthy dove.

food elements: fats, proteins, carbohydrates, vitamins, minerals, and water. Fats, proteins, and carbohydrates supply energy and contain essential nutrients such as vitamins and minerals. Water cools the body, removes waste, and transports nutrients to cells.

The next step is translating the various elements that belong in a healthy diet into practical food choices. Doves are classified as either seed-eating species or fruit-eating species. The fruit-eating species are rare and should not be available as pets, so your pet dove is most likely a seed eater. This does not mean that seeds are all they eat. In reality, a seed-only diet can be deficient in many of the nutrients your pet needs to remain healthy. Although seed mixes should form the bulk of your bird's diet, you can add fresh foods if your bird will accept them. In the wild, doves eat seeds, insects, berries, fruits, green leaves, and plant shoots. In captivity, you must provide your pet with a variety of appealing and nutritious foods.

TIP

Important Points

✔ Offer a variety of seeds to keep your bird in optimal health.

✔ Buy only the freshest seeds and grains available. If they looks dusty, or smell moldy or rancid, throw them out and shop elsewhere.

✔ Never feed seeds that are contaminated by mice or other vermin. Bug-ridden seeds are not harmful, and the bugs can actually offer your bird a high-protein insect treat. However, you risk infesting your house. If you notice insect larvae, moths, or beetles in a bag of seeds, you can freeze it for 24 hours, which should kill most bugs.

✔ Always keep fresh, clean water available for your bird.

A Food Pyramid for Doves

You might want to begin by visualizing a food pyramid that is designed just for doves. At the base of the pyramid are the foods that should make up the bulk of your pet's diet: a variety of nutritious seeds and grains. This can include whole-grain breads, pastas, or other cooked grains; legumes (peas, beans, and peanuts); and shelled nuts in addition to a high-quality seed mix. Next on the pyramid could be manufactured diets, otherwise known as pellets. These are ground-up mixtures of seeds, grains, oils, vitamins, minerals, and other ingredients that are pressed into pellet form or cooked and extruded like dry dog or cat food. Although these diets work very well as the base diet for parrots and some other pet birds, doves usually do best when pellets are used as an addition, rather than as a replacement, for the basic seed diet. It is up to you if you choose to add these to the food you offer your pet.

A little higher up the pyramid sit fruits, vegetables, and dark leafy greens. Most doves relish the daily addition of fresh food into their diets. You can have fun experimenting to see which ones your bird will enjoy. Always rinse these foods carefully before offering them to your pet. Remove uneaten portions after a few hours, because fresh food is an ideal breeding ground for bacteria. If you notice that your bird has loose or runny droppings after eating these high-water-content foods, you might cut back to feeding these treats just three or four times a week. Of course, if your bird has loose droppings and has not eaten any of these foods within the past day, or if it appears fluffed up and lethargic, your dove is displaying serious signs of illness. You should contact your avian veterinarian immediately.

Near the top of the pyramid are animal proteins, which can include hard-boiled eggs, tiny bits of well-cooked meat, and live insects such as mealworms (available in most pet stores). These are a wonderful source of complete protein for your dove and are especially valuable for birds that are breeding and rearing chicks. However, as their position on the pyramid illustrates, these foods should be fed in moderation. Use caution, especially with mealworms. Although they are often a favored treat of doves, they have an exoskeleton made of chitin that is sometimes hard to digest. Limit your pet to no more than a few each day, or they might cause digestive upsets.

Finally, at the tip of the pyramid are dietary supplements, which include products such as vitamin and mineral preparations, calcium powder, grit, probiotics, spirulina, bee pollen, and a host of other proven and not-so-proven nutritional additives. These will be discussed in more detail later. However, keep in mind that these are meant to *supplement* a healthy diet, not compensate for the lack of one.

From General to Specific

Your dove's ideal diet might be influenced by external factors such as temperature and environmental stressors. For example, birds kept in cold conditions require more calories than birds kept at more moderate temperatures. Therefore, it is impossible to detail every circumstance you might encounter. Here is where a little common sense comes in. If your dove is highly active, stressed, sick, molting, or breeding, it will need more food and nutrients than a bird that is sedate, healthy, and not breeding.

Observe your pet's food intake and general level of well-being, discuss any special concerns with your avian veterinarian, and adjust the diet accordingly. The following section explores specific food groups in more detail and will help you to choose a diet that will keep your pet healthy for years to come.

Seeds and Grains

A variety of ready-mixed seed blends are on the market for pet doves, and most large pet shops or feed stores should carry one or two choices. If you are unable to find any, you can mix your own by blending individual seeds and grains or adding to a commercial canary or budgie mix. A good seed mix for small to

---

TIP

Macronutrients and Micronutrients

Nutrients are often divided into two groups. Macronutrients are needed in relatively large amounts. Micronutrients (or trace nutrients) are just as vital but are needed in only very tiny amounts.

---

medium doves such as Diamonds or Ringnecks can include millet, canary seed, milo, wheat, oat groats, safflower, hemp, rapeseed, buckwheat, flax, and hulled sunflower chips. In general, the smallest species (such as Diamond Doves) prefer the smaller seeds. They will happily eat finch or budgie mixes consisting of various millets, canary seed, flax, and niger (thistle) seed. Medium to large dove species appreciate the addition of larger items like shelled peanuts and field peas.

You can experiment with different mixes to see which your pet prefers. Always try to offer a variety of seeds to prevent your dove from feeding selectively on just one or two items and narrowing its food choices. Unlike parrots and most other pet birds that hull their seeds, doves swallow the entire seed, hull and all. This makes it a lot easier to see exactly what is being eaten without having to sift through seed husks and partially eaten grains. As mentioned earlier, if your dove is kept outdoors in cool temperatures, or is breeding or molting, you can offer a higher percentage of high-fat seeds and nuts, such as hulled sunflower or peanut pieces. Conversely, pets kept in smaller indoor cages without a great deal of exercise should get very limited amounts of these high-fat items or they will become obese. An average dove mix will supply between 10–15 percent protein and 2–10 percent fat. This should form the basis of a healthy diet.

Pellets and Extruded Diets

In aviculture, the term *pellets* is often used as a blanket term to describe a wide variety of formulated diets, encompassing a wide range of quality and manufacturing processes. A lot of research has been done on formulated diets for parrots, poultry, and game birds, and these diets are used with much success in those species. Unfortunately, doves and pigeons have not benefited from the same amount of research. Purina Nutri-blend Pigeon pellets are suitable for Ringneck Doves and are designed especially for pigeon and dove species. Many dove keepers offer their birds a dish of game bird pellets or crumbles as a supplement to the basic diet. This can be a great way to add some extra nutrients into your pets' diets, especially when they are breeding or feeding babies. Just do not rely on pellets as a primary food source, at least until a reliable dove-specific pellet is developed and well tested.

Fruits and Vegetables

Fruits and vegetables can be a wonderful source of vitamins, minerals, and antioxidants that can enhance your dove's health. As mentioned earlier, seed-eating doves cannot tolerate large amounts of these high-water-content foods without experiencing minor digestive upsets. However, a daily treat of some carefully chosen fresh food is fine for most birds.

When picking produce to offer your pet, think bright colors for the healthiest choices. For example, sweet potatoes are more nutritious than white potatoes, red peppers have more vitamins than green peppers, red grapes are higher in antioxidants than green grapes, and so on. Dark leafy greens such as spinach, kale, dandelion, and collard greens are nutritional powerhouses, but iceberg lettuce is almost completely devoid of nutrients.

Some dove favorites include shredded greens, grated carrots, finely chopped broccoli florets, diced apple, berries, and fresh corn and peas. Of course, your bird might not like all of these items. With a little experimenting and patience, though, you should find several that become favored food items!

As a word of caution, some dove fanciers recommend feeding a variety of sprouted seeds, but sprouts can be trouble. Even fresh, carefully tended sprouts can harbor dangerous pathogens like *Escherichia coli* or salmonella bacteria, which are deadly to your pet. If you do feed sprouts, use only the freshest available and rinse them repeatedly before giving to your bird.

Live Food and Other Animal Proteins

Although live foods (insects) are not strictly necessary for your dove, they do offer a good source of protein. Additionally, most doves relish the treat. Your local pet store probably carries a variety of these insects, including mealworms, crickets, wax worms, and king mealworms (sold as Superworms). You can also purchase dried insects if you are squeamish about handling live bugs. Mealworms are most

Malnutrition is one of the most common, yet least recognized, killers of pet birds. Feed your dove properly to keep your pet healthy and disease free.

favored by doves, and you can offer a few in your pet's dish as a special treat. One warning: if your pet does not eat them and they escape into your house, mealworms grow into large, black beetles. They are not harmful. However, you might want to monitor your dove carefully when feeding these to prevent escapees from getting out of the cage.

Another good source of protein is chopped hard-boiled eggs. This is especially important for breeding doves that are raising chicks. You can crush the eggshells and mix them with the egg, which will provide your bird a great source of calcium along with the protein. Just be certain to boil the eggs thoroughly. Uncooked or partially cooked eggs can harbor bacteria that could sicken your pet. Some doves enjoy very tiny pieces of thoroughly cooked meat or bits of cheese, but these should be fed only rarely and as special treats. Birds lack the enzyme to digest milk proteins such as cheese properly, so large or frequent amounts can upset their digestive system.

Never feed your bird avocado, raw rhubarb, chocolate, or onions. These all contain certain compounds that might be harmful to birds. Finally, never let your bird consume alcohol, caffeine, tobacco, or large amounts of sugar or salt. Alcohol and caffeine are dangerous for birds, as are large doses of sugar or salt. Nicotine is a deadly poison. Numerous reports describe pet birds dying after pecking at cigarette filters carelessly left in ashtrays. In captivity, your dove is completely dependent upon

you for its safety and welfare. Please make wise choices to provide it with a healthy environment.

Supplements

As stressed throughout this chapter, a healthy diet should go a long way toward supplying all the nutrients your pet needs. A vitamin/mineral supplement given once or twice a week, however, will provide a little extra assurance that all those needs are indeed being met, especially if your bird is a finicky eater. Most vitamin supplements designed for pet birds are fine, although Nekton Corporation does make a vitamin/mineral product specifically designed for doves and pigeons. Some folks even use poultry vitamins, which are usually cheaper.

Feeding the Supplements

Although the instructions on most bird vitamins claim you can mix them in the water, this is not a good idea. First of all, vitamins in water can settle to the bottom or lose their potency very quickly. Secondly, most (but not all) vitamin supplements use a form of sugar as a carrier for the vitamins and minerals. Putting this into the water can quickly turn the water into a dangerous bacterial soup. It is best to sprinkle the supplement onto soft food, such as chopped eggs or moist fruits and vegetables. Do not sprinkle it onto the seed, as it will not adhere and will simply sift to the bottom. If you do choose to add the supplement to water, make sure you never let the water sit for more than 24 hours before changing.

Grit

In addition to vitamin/mineral supplements, your dove will require a small amount of grit to help it digest its food. Unlike other birds that hull their seed and discard the husk, doves swallow their seeds whole. The seed passes into their muscular stomach, where it mixes with grit to grind it up. Experts cannot agree on how much or what kind of grit is best for doves. Some even question whether domestic doves (which are fed a more easily digested diet than that typically eaten by wild birds) require grit at all. You can offer your bird two kinds of grit. Distinguishing between them is important. Indigestible grit is sand or small bits of ground rock. Offer this cautiously, as sick birds can sometimes overeat it and cause inter-

nal impactions. Digestible grit, such as oyster shell, ground cuttlebone, or crushed eggshells, is calcium based and can be kept in your bird's cage at all times. This type of grit will pass through its system safely and offers an excellent dose of calcium as well. Powdered calcium supplements are a valuable addition to the diet of breeding birds, who have a much higher need for calcium than nonbreeding pets. You can purchase these at a well-stocked pet shop or feed store or from numerous catalog or Internet bird supply companies.

Other Supplements

Numerous other supplements and remedies, both human and pet grade, are sometimes used with birds. Most of these are available from pet supply companies or human health food stores. Some of these can be helpful, some are unproven, and some are downright dangerous. Always use caution, and call your veterinarian if you have any questions.

Probiotics: These are various species of the healthy bacteria that populate your bird's digestive tract and help to break down food, extract nutrients, and fight off disease. Yogurt and other cultured dairy products are a great source of probiotics for humans, but these bacteria are believed to be somewhat species specific. That means that the forms that live in human digestive tracts might not be able to live in avian systems and vice versa. A few bird-specific probiotics are now on the market, and these might be a healthy addition to your bird's diet. Probiotics are especially valuable if your pet has been on antibiotic therapy, which kills good bacteria along with the bad.

Digestive enzymes: Like probiotics, digestive enzymes help the body extract nutrients from food. These can be very helpful to a sick bird that is having trouble digesting food, but there is some disagreement about whether or not they offer any benefit to a healthy bird. They are safe to use, however, and will not cause your bird any harm.

Charcoal: Often touted as a blood purifier, charcoal moves through the digestive tract, absorbing all sorts of things, including nutrients. Charcoal might be fed to birds for a few legitimate reasons, mostly to counteract ingested poisons, but you should never give it to your pet except under veterinary supervision.

Over-the-counter (OTC) antibiotics and other "remedies": If your bird is ill, take it to an experienced avian veterinarian and follow his or her instructions. *Never* give your bird the antibiotics or other treatments you can purchase without a prescription at the pet store. First of all, if you do not know exactly what is wrong with your pet, you can do a lot of damage by feeding it unnecessary or inappropriate drugs. Secondly, even if you could somehow identify the specific pathogen that was sickening your bird, it is unlikely that any OTC medicine would cure it. Over time, bacteria build up resistances to commonly used drugs, creating the need for new or different formulations. Most of the OTC antibiotics available are weak or completely ineffective against most pathogenic (dangerous) bacteria and will only harm your bird more by killing off the good bacteria

TIP

Important Reminders
✔ Always wash fresh produce thoroughly before offering to your bird.
✔ Never feed your pet produce that is moldy, discolored, or otherwise past its prime. If you do not want to eat it, do not expect your bird to do so.
✔ Remove uneaten fresh food after three to four hours, before bacteria begin to grow and multiply.
✔ If your dove experiences loose or runny stools after eating fruits or vegetables, cut back on the amount or frequency of these offerings.

in its system. The same goes for antifungals, dewormers, and other products designed to treat parasites or disease. Do not use these products unless directed by your veterinarian, or you risk harming or even killing your pet.

Although this might all sound a little complicated, it really isn't. Doves, unlike parrots, actually do quite well on a seed-only diet, as long as you provide a good-quality seed mix and a vitamin/mineral supplement. The addition of fresh foods and protein sources can help round out your pet's diet and give you the opportunity to offer a few special treats.

KEEPING YOUR DOVE HEALTHY

Doves are by nature hardy and long-lived birds, so with proper care your pet should be around to keep you company for many, many years. Remember that good husbandry is the foundation for keeping your dove healthy.

Clean cages, nutritious food, fresh water, good air quality, and plenty of natural light will help prevent many of the illnesses that befall pet birds. If your dove becomes ill or gets injured despite your efforts, you must respond quickly and appropriately to the problem and provide whatever veterinary care your pet requires.

Choosing a Veterinarian

If you have other pets, you might already have a great veterinarian. Unfortunately, the veterinarian who treats your dog or cat will probably not be the best choice for your bird. Birds are obviously quite different from mam-

Birds kept outdoors are exposed to many more diseases and parasites than those housed indoors.

mals, and veterinarians usually specialize in certain types of animals. You will want to find one who specializes in birds or at least sees a number of birds daily in practice. Avian specialists are usually easy to find in large cities, especially in the Sunbelt states, but might be harder to come by in rural areas. To find one in your area, ask local bird breeders or pet shops for recommendations or contact the Association of Avian Vets (AAV) at (561) 393-8901 or online at *www.aav.org*

The best time to find a veterinarian is before you need one. Do not wait until your pet is desperately ill to start flipping through the phone book in search of a qualified practitioner. Ideally, you should decide how you will provide veterinary care before you even bring your pet home. Talk to the veterinarian and find out fee schedules, hours, and how after-hours emergencies are handled. Some clinics provide

24-hour emergency care, while others will direct you to different facilities. In either case, be certain to keep a list of emergency phone numbers in a handy place for ready access.

Birds are masters at hiding symptoms of disease or injury. As prey animals, a noticeably weak or hurt member of the flock is a tempting target for predators. For that reason, an ailing bird will struggle with its last ounce of strength to keep up with the flock and appear normal. By the time it is too sick or weak to keep up the facade, it is probably near death. That is why you, as your bird's guardian, must be aware of any subtle changes in its behavior that might signify illness.

Signs of a Sick Bird

If your pet exhibits any of the following problems, contact your veterinarian immediately.

✔ Appears listless, feathers ruffled, sleeps excessively.

✔ Unkempt or missing feathers, soiled vent feathers.

✔ Dull or cloudy eyes, partially closed eyes, any eye discharge or swelling.

✔ Open mouth breathing, unusual rasping or clicking sounds while breathing, tail bobs up and down while breathing, nasal discharge.

✔ Loss of appetite, change in frequency or appearance of droppings that cannot be attributed to recent food item.

✔ Lameness, drooped wing, or bleeding.

Most importantly, be observant and learn what is normal for your pet. A very temporary change in behavior might just signify a bird that is tired, stressed, or depressed. However, if behavioral changes last more than a day, or if your bird shows any of the previous symptoms, call your veterinarian.

Dove Diseases

Diseases typically fall into one of five categories: bacterial, viral, fungal, parasitic, and protozoal. As mentioned earlier, simply keeping your pet's cage and dishes clean and feeding a healthy diet can avoid many of these problems. To understand why husbandry is so critical, it helps to understand how diseases are transmitted.

Some diseases are carried as airborne particles and infect a new host when they are breathed in or otherwise ingested. For example, a sick bird might pass the infection through its droppings or feather dust, which dry and get blown around in the air. Other diseases might be tracked into your home or your pet's cage by other pets, insects, or rodents. Still others might hitch a ride on your clothing, hair, or hands and infect your pet when you handle it. Bacteria and fungi thrive on spoiled food or in dirty water.

As you can see, germs are everywhere. However, proper and frequent cleaning will go a long way toward protecting your dove from the pathogens. This is not to imply that you must spend every spare moment wiping up each speck of dust. Do make sure, though, that you thoroughly clean the bird's food and water dishes each day, clean the cage bottom daily, and give the rest of the cage a good scrubbing at least once a week (or more often as necessary, especially in hot weather). Pay special attention to perches and other surfaces that the bird stands on, as droppings often foul these. See the chapter "Housing Your Pet Dove" for more information on cleaning and disinfection.

Bacterial Diseases

Doves are susceptible to many of the same bacterial diseases as humans and other pets, so be certain you wash your hands before and after handling your bird. The following are some of the most common bacteria that can sicken your dove.

Salmonella: Pet reptiles, wild birds, and house-flies or other insects can carry various species of *Salmonella* bacteria. Salmonella can infect your dove and cause either an acute illness that is characterized by life-threatening diarrhea, loss of appetite, dehydration, and lethargy, or it can appear in a chronic form that causes arthritis, loss of balance, and damage to the liver, kidneys, heart, and spleen. A bird that has the chronic form can pass the bacteria through its eggs and infect its chicks. Humans can also contract the disease, especially the elderly or immune compromised. So you must seek proper treatment for your pet. Your veterinarian can prescribe appropriate antibiotics to fight the infection. Adding *Lactobacillus* bacteria (the healthy bacteria found in yogurt) to its diet also might help your bird fight the disease and regain strength. Lactobacillus supplements are available in many pet stores or health food stores.

Pasteurella bacteria can be found in most rodents and many wild birds, but one of the most common sources of this pathogen is the family cat. Cats almost always carry these bacteria in their saliva, and they are deadly to birds. If your dove is ever bitten or scratched by a cat, even if the scratch is so minor it can hardly be seen, get your pet to a veterinarian immediately for antibiotic therapy, or it will almost surely die. Pasteurella causes severe respiratory disease, diarrhea, and possible liver and spleen damage.

═══════════ **T I P** ═══════════

Remember to Quarantine

You can avoid the spread of many diseases by remembering to quarantine all new birds you bring into your home. Review the section about quarantining in the chapter "Choosing Your Pet Dove" for specifics and consider vaccinating your pets as recommended by your veterinarian.

The enterobacteria group includes a number of different bacteria that are normally present in the intestinal tract of mammals (including humans) and some species of birds. The most commonly known of these is *Escherichia coli*, or *E. coli* for short. *E.coli* can cause severe gastrointestinal or systemic disease in doves. Symptoms include lethargy, ruffled feathers, diarrhea, refusal to eat, and dehydration. Less frequently it can cause respiratory problems, nasal discharge, or genital tract infections. If the disease is caught in time, prompt treatment with antibiotics can save your bird.

Chlamydiosis—also known as psittacosis, ornithosis, or parrot fever—is a deadly disease caused by a bacterium known as *Chlamydia psittaci*. Symptoms of chlamydiosis include listlessness, loss of appetite, bright green or yellow urates (the normally white portion of a bird's droppings), and nasal or ocular discharge. Chlamydiosis is highly contagious among birds and can infect humans as well. In humans, it causes a flu-like disease that is treatable with antibiotics. Healthy adults are rarely at risk, but

the elderly and immune-compromised should avoid possible exposure. In birds, prompt treatment with the appropriate antibiotics can save an infected bird, but untreated individuals usually will not survive.

Chlamydiosis transmits mostly from bird to bird, therefore your pet is unlikely to catch this disease unless it is exposed to other birds. You can, however, transmit the disease to your pet if you handle a sick bird in a pet shop or at a bird fair and then come home and handle your pet. Always shower and change clothes after attending bird fairs or visiting pet shops or aviaries, or at least wash your hands thoroughly before touching your pet, its cage, or its dishes.

Viral Diseases

Assuming your bird was healthy when you purchased it and it has not been exposed to other sick birds, viral diseases are less likely to be a problem. Viruses are usually (but not always) spread from bird to bird, so a single pet bird will not have the same exposure to viruses as a bird living in a communal flock.

Paramyxovirus: There are numerous serotypes of Paramyxovirus and these viruses are capable of causing a wide variety of disease in most bird species. The most important form that affects pet birds is known as NDV, or Newcastle disease. Newcastle disease can cause many different symptoms depending on the strain. Typical symptoms include greenish diarrhea, difficulty breathing, eye or nasal discharge, tremors, convulsions, and paralysis. The virus is usually fatal, but some birds do survive. Newcastle disease is highly contagious and deadly to poultry. It can cause mild illness, usually conjunctivitis (eye inflammation), in humans. A vaccine is developed for poultry that can protect your dove from this disease, so be sure to discuss the risks and benefits with your veterinarian.

Another serotype of Paramyxovirus is known as pigeon paramyxovirus-1 (PPMV-1). This form affects mostly pigeons and doves, especially those who come in contact with wild birds. Symptoms are similar to those of Newcastle disease, but this form of the disease usually does not cause severe illness in poultry and does not seem to affect humans at all. Because it is deadly to doves and pigeons, your veterinarian will probably recommend vaccination, especially if you keep your bird outdoors.

Poxvirus, or pigeon pox, is spread mostly by mosquitoes. The disease can take several forms

It is much easier to avoid disease than to treat it once it has occurred. Keep your pet's cage clean, and quarantine any new birds you bring into the house.

and is highly fatal. In the dry form of the disease, birds develop large wartlike growths on their face, feet, legs, beak, or eyelids. These lesions ulcerate, scab, and bleed profusely if disturbed. In the wet form, which attacks primarily the mucous membranes, yellowish lesions appear in the mouth, throat, esophagus, crop, or trachea. Some birds can have symptoms of both the wet and dry form at the same time. A vaccine is available to prevent the virus.

Fungal Diseases

Fungal diseases rarely cause problems for a healthy bird living in clean surroundings. When they do occur, they are often secondary to other diseases or a result of poor husbandry.

Fungi spores are everywhere in our environment. Normally, your pet's immune system fights them off quite effectively, and routine cleaning temporarily removes the spores from surfaces. If debris and litter are allowed to build up, especially in warm, humid conditions, the spores will grow and multiply rapidly. They will soon reach overwhelming numbers. If your pet's immune system is already stressed from other pathogens or from poor nutrition, the fungi can take hold and cause disease.

Most people understand that visible mold is a fungus. What they do not understand is that many fungi, and the toxins they produce, are invisible to the naked eye. Even if an area looks clean, a musty or rancid smell is a strong indication that fungi are present in unhealthy numbers, and your pet is at risk.

Aspergillosis: A fungus known as *Aspergillus fumigatus* causes the most common form of this deadly respiratory disease. Symptoms of aspergillosis may include difficulty breathing, coughing, wheezing, weight loss, and depression. Various drugs can treat the infection, but treatment is long, difficult, and not always successful. Preventing the infection is much easier by conscientious cleaning than is treating a bird suffering from the disease.

Candidiasis is caused by opportunistic yeast known as *Candida albicans*. This yeast attacks the bird's gastrointestinal tract, most commonly the crop. Sometimes the characteristic white plaques associated with the disease are visible in the bird's mouth, appearing somewhat like bits of cottage cheese. Usually a thick mucus is present, which may or may not have a strong odor. Symptoms of the disease are vomiting, depression, loss of appetite, and weight loss. Candidiasis is easily treatable with medication if caught early, but untreated birds can die from it. It can be caused by spoiled or moldy feed but it often occurs secondary to another infection. For example, the prolonged use of antibiotics to fight a bacterial infection can leave your bird vulnerable to candidiasis. Your veterinarian might recommend adding an antifungal drug as a preventative measure during antibiotic therapy.

Parasites

Parasites come in many forms, ranging from the familiar ticks, fleas, and worms that plague our pet dogs and cats to microscopic organisms that infect the blood or intestinal tract. In general, healthy birds that are kept indoors rarely have problems with parasites. Do not attempt to treat your bird for parasites unless a veterinarian has diagnosed them or you are otherwise certain what you are dealing with. Many of the "remedies" sold over the counter for parasites are dangerous and unnecessary, including mite and lice sprays and "cage protector" devices, which usually contain harmful chemicals and can cause liver damage.

If your birds are kept outdoors, parasites do pose a greater threat. Talk with your veterinarian to evaluate which parasites are most common to your area and what measures you should take to treat your birds.

Mites, lice, and fleas: These parasites are usually host specific, which means the fleas that infest your dog should not pose much of a threat to your dove. In rare cases, lice and fleas will make their home in bird feathers. However, these are easily treated with a very light dusting of pyrethrin powder, which is used for flea control on puppies and kittens. If fleas and lice are a problem in the aviary, pyrethrin powder can also be used to kill parasites hiding in cage crevices or along baseboards. Mites are a little trickier. Many species of mites are avian specific and are specific to certain areas of a bird's body. Some mites are external and live in the feathers and skin of infected birds. Others move internally and infect the respiratory system of the bird. Feather and skin mites can cause itching, scratching, patchy loss of feathers, and scaly skin lesions. Mites in the respiratory system can cause coughing, sneezing, nasal discharge, and difficulty breathing. These are all curable, but proper identification and treatment is the key.

Worms: Various types of worms can infect doves, but worms are most common in flocks kept outdoors. Indoor pets are rarely infected. Tapeworms are most common in birds that have access to the ground, where the worms live during part of their life cycle. Tapeworms live in the bird's digestive tract and steal nutrients. A minor infection might not cause any obvious symptoms, but a severe infection can cause signs of malnutrition, weight loss, and diarrhea.

Roundworms live primarily in the digestive tract but can also live on the surface of the eye and in body cavities or air sacs. Symptoms include weight loss, anorexia, depression, and diarrhea.

Threadworms are tiny worms that burrow into the lining of the intestinal tract, crop, or esophagus. Symptoms include vomiting, depression, diarrhea (sometimes bloody), weight loss, and hemorrhaging in the crop and esophagus.

Flukes are flatworms that typically live in the bile ducts or liver. Symptoms include weight loss, depression, anemia, and elevated liver enzymes. All of these parasites can be successfully treated once they are properly identified but can cause death if left untreated.

Protozoal Infections

Protozoal infections are caused by microscopic parasites that most commonly attack the gastrointestinal or respiratory tract but can also affect the heart, liver, or other organs. The two parasites that most commonly affect doves are *Coccidia* and *Trichomonas*. Trichomoniasis is commonly referred to as canker, and it is spread through direct contact with an infected bird or through contaminated food or water. This is another disease that can usually be avoided through good sanitation and quarantine practices. The infection usually settles in the mouth, crop, esophagus, or trachea but can also affect the liver, lungs, and air sacs. Symptoms include weight loss, vomiting, and difficulty breathing. Sometimes the yellowish plaques caused by the parasite are visible in the bird's mouth.

Coccidiosis is also spread through contaminated food and water. Coccidia parasites are usually intestinal but can also infect the liver, kidneys, and lungs. Symptoms include depression, diarrhea (sometimes bloody or filled with mucus), anemia, and loss of appetite. Protozoal infections are curable if diagnosed early and treated properly.

As you probably noticed while reading about the various diseases that can affect your dove, the symptoms for many diseases are the same. That is why it is so important to have your bird examined by a qualified veterinarian at the first signs of illness. Diagnosing the problem yourself with any certainty is nearly impossible. Never give your pet over-the-counter "bird remedies" unless recommended by your veterinarian. Most of these are useless at best and might even worsen your pet's illness. The same goes for human medicines or medicines pre-

Your bird will not instinctively recognize the dangers present in an average home. It will depend on you to protect it from harm.

scribed for other pets. Many of these can be toxic to birds. If you do not know exactly what you are dealing with, you could make the problem much worse or even kill your dove.

Household Dangers and Accidents

Although a healthy dove in clean surroundings is unlikely to experience any of the above diseases, accidents and injuries are another story. The average household is filled with potential dangers for your pet, and you must keep your bird safe. The following are just some of the areas to keep an eye on.

Other pets: No matter how tame and gentle you think your animals are, please do not ignore their predatory instincts. Have you ever thrown a ball for your dog to fetch or dragged a string across the floor for your cat to pounce on? Your dog or cat will likely have the same reaction to a fluttering dove. Even if they do not intend to harm the bird, their size and strength alone make them a great danger. Ferrets and snakes are natural predators of birds and will see your dove as simply another tasty snack. Never take your dove out of its cage if other animals are present; lock them securely in another room before you allow your bird to come out and enjoy some free time.

Children: Children, especially the very young, almost always love animals and want to pick them up, pet them, and cuddle. Doves are gentle creatures and make a fine pet for youngsters, provided the child has been shown how to handle a bird properly. Always supervise, for both the bird's safety and the child's.

Open containers of water: This includes aquariums, toilet bowls, buckets, and cooking pots. Doves fly beautifully, but they are lousy swimmers. If your pet accidentally falls into water, it will not be able to get out and will drown. Once again, always supervise free flight time.

Household poisons: The average household is filled with toxins, including cleaning products, paints, pesticides, and poisonous plants. Do not allow your bird to touch any of these items. As a rule of thumb, if you would not want to put it into your mouth, do not let your dove eat it!

Airborne toxins: Aerosol sprays, cooking fumes, and fumes from household chemicals such as paint thinner, varnish, and cleaning supplies can cause respiratory failure and death in your pet. Always move your bird to another room when you are using products of this sort, and open a window if possible to ventilate the area. Overheated Teflon cookware produces an odorless, invisible gas that is highly toxic to birds. Be aware of Teflon not just in pans but also on other surfaces, including irons, drip pans, and toaster ovens.

Ceiling fans, mirrors, and windows: These are all a hazard if your dove flies into them. Turn off ceiling fans when your dove is out of its cage, and close blinds or drapes if possible so your bird does not fly into windows. Throw a towel over large mirrors so your pet does not mistake them for an open window. Of course, make sure all windows and doors are securely closed so that your bird cannot escape.

Although this might all sound a little overwhelming, it is really just a matter of common sense. If you have other pets or if you have children, it is probably second nature for you to keep an eye open for dangers and remove them from the reach of inquisitive hands or paws.

Common Poisonous Household Plants

Aloe

Amaryllis

Asian Lily (Liliaceae)

Asparagus Fern

Autumn Crocus

Avocado

Azalea

Bird of Paradise

American Bittersweet

European Bittersweet

Branching Ivy

Buckeye

Caladium

Calla Lily

Chinaberry Tree

Chinese Evergreen

Christmas Rose

Clematis

Corn Plant (aka Cornstalk Plant)

Cutleaf Philodendron (aka Ceriman)

Cyclamen

Daffodil

Day Lily

Dumb Cane

Easter Lily

Elephant Ears

English Ivy

Fiddle-Leaf Philodendron

Foxglove

Gladiolas

Glory Lily

Gold Dieffenbachia

Gold Dust Dracaena

Golden Pothos

Heartleaf Philodendron

Heavenly Bamboo

Holly

Horsehead Philodendron

Hyacinth

Hydrangea

Iris

Japanese Yew (aka Yew)

Jerusalem Cherry

Kalanchoe

Lily of the Valley

Madagascar Dragon Tree

Mauna Loa Peace Lily (aka Peace Lily)

Mexican Breadfruit

Mistletoe "American"

Morning Glory

Mother-in-Law

Narcissus

Onion

Peace Lily (aka Mauna Loa Peace Lily)

Philodendron Pertusum

Plumosa Fern

Rhododendron

Sago Palm

Satin Pothos

Schefflera

Spotted Dumb Cane

Stargazer Lily

Striped Dracaena

Sweetheart Ivy

Taro Vine

Tiger Lily

Tomato Plant

Tree Philodendron

Tulip

Variable Dieffenbachia

Variegated Philodendron

Warneckei Dracaena

Yucca

Adapted from the ASPCA/National Animal Poison Control Center

Always keep a pet carrier suitable for birds on hand for emergency trips to the veterinarian. Pet carriers will also work as temporary hospital cages in a pinch.

Emergencies

In an emergency, your dove's survival will depend on how quickly you react and how prepared you are. Always keep a list of emergency phone numbers handy, including your veterinarian's daytime and after-hours emergency phone, Poison Control Hotline, and the phone numbers of any local breeders or bird clubs that might offer valuable advice in a pinch.

You should also have a bird first aid kit on hand. (Most of the items will work for any species of pet emergency.) Although you can buy ready-made animal first aid kits, you can easily assemble a more complete and specialized kit on your own. I use a large plastic toolbox with a removable tray, but any container or cabinet space dedicated to the purpose is fine. Your kit should include:

✔ Clean towels for catching and restraining a bird.

✔ Gauze pads or rolled gauze.

✔ Vetrap, which is a stretchy bandaging tape that clings to itself without adhesive, so it will not damage feathers. It is available from some large pet shops or from your vet.

✔ Cotton balls and swabs.

✔ A pair of small sharp scissors for clipping feathers or cutting bandages.

✔ Tweezers.

✔ Small needle-nosed pliers for pulling bleeding feathers.

✔ Nail clippers for trimming nails. Cat claw clippers work great for doves.

✔ Eyedropper or disposable pipettes.

✔ Penlight.

✔ Heating pad.

✔ Styptic powder.

✔ Hydrogen peroxide solution.

✔ Povidone-iodine solution (Betadine) for treating minor wounds.

✔ Sterile saline solution for flushing wounds or foreign bodies in the eye.

✔ Electrolyte solution (Pedialite) for preventing and treating dehydration.

With the above supplies on hand, you will be prepared for almost any emergency that comes your way. You should also keep a bird overnight bag in case a disaster forces you to evacuate your home. In addition to the above first aid kit, keep a travel carrier stocked with bottled water, a sealed bag of your pet's food, and dishes. In an evacuation, you could simply place your bird into the carrier and you would be ready to go.

Finding a good veterinarian is the first step to ensure your dove's long-term health.

Wild doves suffer from predation and habitat destruction in many countries.

Birds are prey animals and hide the symptoms of illness as long as possible to keep up with the flock.

Do not allow your pet dove to fly free outdoors. It will not have the homing instincts that some species of pigeon are famous for, and it will likely be lost.

This beautiful Nicobar pigeon has unique long neck feathers known as "hackles." These give the bird a striking appearance.

Always observe your pet carefully for subtle signs of illness. Once you know what is normal for your dove, you will be more likely to spot trouble at an early stage.

The first step in an emergency is to remain calm and assess the situation. Usually the best thing you can do is get the bird to a veterinarian immediately, but you can do some things to stabilize the bird until you reach the veterinarian. You will need to determine what has caused the injury. Did another animal attack your pet? Is your dove bleeding? Does it appear to have broken bones? Is it unconscious? In shock? Once you have identified the problem, you can take action.

Shock

In most cases of injury, sudden illness, or shock, the most important thing you can do is keep the bird warm. Place it on top of a towel in a travel carrier, empty aquarium, or cardboard box on top of a heating pad. Place the pad so that only half the container is on the heating pad—that way, the bird can move to a cooler spot if it becomes overheated. Cover the top of the container loosely with a towel, and contact your veterinarian. If the dove is bleeding, you will need to stop the bleeding. Otherwise, handle the bird as little as possible. Birds in shock are in a very precarious state, and the stress of handling might worsen their condition.

Bleeding

First you must find the source of the bleeding. This sounds obvious, but telling where the blood is coming from is not always easy. Birds have what are called blood feathers—these are new feathers that have not emerged from their sheaths yet and are still growing and filled with blood. If one of these breaks off, it can bleed profusely, and your dove might be spattered with blood although there is no obvious injury. Damaged beaks or torn toenails are another common source of bleeding. Of course, an injury such as a dog or cat bite might also be the cause of bleeding. If there is just a small amount of visible blood, the bird seems alert, and the wound was not caused by another animal, simply putting it back into its cage and observing it closely might be best. Healthy doves have a good blood-clotting mechanism, and the bleeding might stop shortly on its own if the bird is not panicked or struggling. If the bleeding does not stop after a few minutes or if the bird appears weak, you will have to intervene.

For profuse bleeding or bleeding that will not stop, hold gentle but steady pressure against the area. If blood is coming from a broken toenail or minor beak damage, apply a dab of styptic powder to the spot and hold gentle pressure. Do not get the styptic powder into the bird's eyes or mouth. In the case of a broken blood feather, styptic powder often will not work because the hollow feather shaft acts as a capillary tube and continues to draw blood out. If it continues to bleed, you will need to pull out the damaged feather. To do so, gently restrain your pet in a towel, and spread out its wing. Grasp the wing firmly at a spot right above the damaged feather. Using needle-nosed pliers, grasp the feather shaft near where it emerges from the skin, and pull steadily in the direction of feather growth. Once the feather is out, apply

If your pet breaks its wing, gently fold the wing against its body and immobilize the wing with Vetrap tape until you reach the veterinarian's office.

pressure for a minute or so to the follicle to prevent bleeding.

If the bleeding was caused by an animal bite or other trauma, your pet might have internal injuries that are not obvious. You can carefully flush the wound with saline solution and then cleanse with hydrogen peroxide solution. Use a cotton ball or gauze to apply povidone-iodine solution, and hold pressure with clean gauze until bleeding stops. Transport the bird to a veterinarian as soon as possible for antibiotic treatment (in the case of animal bites) and a thorough exam to rule out internal injuries.

Broken Bones

Bird bones are incredibly light and strong, but they are not immune to breaking. Do not attempt to treat a broken bone on your own—this is definitely a job for the experts. If your dove has a broken wing, you can attempt to immobilize the wing until you can reach the veterinarian's office. To do so, gently and carefully fold the wing against the bird's body, and wrap a length of Vetrap around the bird, pinning the wing to its body. Do not wrap too tightly or you run the risk of interfering with the bird's breathing. Please note this is only a temporary solution for avoiding further injury while transporting the bird to the veterinarian's office.

Heatstroke

If your dove is kept indoors, it will be comfortable at the same temperatures that you and your family enjoy. For outdoor birds, make sure the cage has shaded areas that the birds can move into to escape the Sun. Never leave your pet's cage in direct sunlight, and never leave your bird (or any other animal) in a car during warm weather, even if the windows are rolled down. If for any reason your pet is suffering from heatstroke, you must act quickly. Signs of

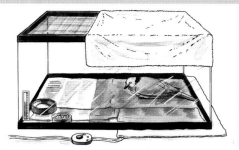

Sick birds deplete their strength trying to maintain body heat, so the most important thing you can do is to provide heat. A small aquarium placed halfway over a heating pad set at low or medium, then draped with a towel, will serve as a hospital cage until you can reach a veterinarian.

heatstroke include open-mouthed panting, holding the wings away from the body, weakness, and loss of balance. Immediately move the bird to a cooler location, and mist it with cool (not cold) water from a misting bottle. Offer a shallow dish of cool water. If the bird seems weak or dehydrated, drip a few drops of electrolyte solution (Pedialyte) into its beak with an eyedropper or pipette. Do not force fluids into the bird or you might aspirate it. If your pet does not recover quickly, call your veterinarian for advice.

Burns

Small minor burns can be treated by running cool water onto the affected area. If the burn is serious or covers a large area, treat the bird for shock and get it to a veterinarian immediately. Never use human ointments on your pet. These ointments will foul and damage the feathers and can cause them to lose their insulating properties. They might also be toxic if your bird ingests them in an attempt to clean its feathers.

These measures are temporary fixes until you can get your bird to a veterinarian.

BREEDING DOVES

Once you get bitten by the dove bug, you might decide to start breeding your pets. Birds are not at all like dogs and cats when it comes to breeding. For starters, they are monogamous and will mate for life.

If its mate dies, a dove will remarry if a suitable mate comes along, but they do take these pairings pretty seriously. Although compatibility is rarely an issue with doves, a new pair will take time to settle down and get used to each other before they begin to breed.

Setting Up a Breeding Pair

The first step in setting up a breeding pair is making sure you have a male and female. Although this sounds obvious, it is not always that easy. Most doves are monomorphic, which means that both males and females look alike. Because birds' sexual organs are internal, there is no obvious visual difference between the sexes. Once the birds reach maturity, you can

Doves are relatively easy to breed, but it still takes a fair amount of work and commitment.

tell by behavior. Until then, determining gender is difficult.

Some folks claim to be able to tell the girls from the boys by the bird's size, head shape, or pelvic width, but these are still simply educated guesses. The only reliable way to determine gender is by laparoscopic exam or through DNA testing.

Sexing Procedures

In a laparoscopic exam, also known as surgical sexing, a veterinarian makes a small incision in the bird's side and looks inside with a tiny viewing device that allows him or her to inspect the sexual organs. In doves, a gender determination can be made by viewing inside the cloaca, or vent of the bird. Both of these methods are invasive and require anesthesia.

The more common method is DNA testing. This test uses a drop of blood (usually drawn from a clipped toenail) or a bit of feather pulp from a shed feather. This method is completely reliable and noninvasive. However, getting results from the laboratory takes a week or so.

A true pair can be set up for breeding when they reach maturity, at about nine to 12 months. Some birds will mature as early as six months of age. However, laying eggs at such a young age can be detrimental to the hen's health. You should wait until the hen is about a year old, but the male can be slightly younger.

Preparing the Cage

Although they need to build a nest, doves are notoriously lacking in nest-building skills. You will have to help them out by offering some nesting containers. Small wooden trays, wicker or plastic canary nests, or shallow baskets all make good nest foundations. If your birds are in a large cage or flight, fasten one or two of these in a high, protected spot in the cage and let them choose. If the birds are in a small indoor cage, you can simply place a nest container on the floor of the cage.

Make sure plenty of unobstructed room is above the perches to allow the birds room to mate. They will need at least 10 inches (25 cm) height above the highest perch and room for the male to flap his wings for balance when he mounts the hen, or breeding attempts might fail. You can add a base of clean pine shavings or straw to the container to cushion the eggs, and place some small twigs nearby. The male might carry small twigs over and drop them into the nest to show the hen what a skillful builder he is. Ringnecks and Diamond Doves prefer open nests, but their nest-building behavior is half-hearted at best.

The Mating Ritual

Males usually begin the ritual by vocalization, emitting a drawn-out cooing sound. He will strut in front of the hen, fan his tail, and bow down rhythmically while cooing repeatedly. This is called the "bow coo" and is an important part of the courtship ritual. Some males will repeatedly reach back and peck themselves behind the wing and then offer their open beak to the hen. This is usually a prelude to mutual preening about the face and bill. The female may crouch and quiver and make begging sounds like a baby bird. Often the male will make regurgitating movements and go through the motions of feeding the hen, who thrusts her beak into his. When the hen is ready, she crouches down and spreads her wings, inviting the male to mount her.

In the actual mating, the hen lifts her tail and the male bends his tail under her, aligning their cloacas. At this point, both birds slightly evert their cloacal tissue, and the male ejaculates and deposits his sperm onto the hen's cloacal tissue. This has been dubbed the "cloacal kiss." Actual copulation usually only lasts a few seconds, but the pair might repeat the process several times in a row.

Once mating has begun, the male will attempt to drive or coax the female into the nest. She might not want to spend a lot of time in the nest in the beginning but will stay there for longer and longer periods as she gets closer to laying. During this time, the male will continue to offer nesting material to the hen, so keep a supply of thin twigs, coconut fibers, or straw on the cage floor for him to choose from. The female lays eggs about 10 days to two weeks after the first mating. However, the birds will probably continue to mate frequently during that time.

Dove Eggs and Incubation

Small doves usually lay one or two eggs per clutch (very rarely three), about one or two days apart. The eggs are white and glossy. They are quite rounded compared with some other bird eggs. You can tell if the eggs are fertile about five days after they begin incubation by candling them. To candle an egg, you simply hold it up and shine a strong flashlight or special candling light through the egg. If they are fertile, you will see red threadlike blood vessels in the egg and a tiny blob that is the developing chick.

Always wash your hands thoroughly before handling eggs, and handle them very gently. Germs can penetrate the shell, and rough movements could kill the fragile embryo. If the parents are nervous and not very tame, resist the urge to poke around the nest or you might frighten them, causing them to desert the nest or damage the eggs.

Egg-Bound Hen

Sometimes the female will have difficulty laying an egg. This is most frequently caused by poor nutrition and can indicate a deficiency of calcium, vitamin D_3, selenium, or vitamin E. It can also occur in very young or very old hens, birds that are overweight, or those that have experienced some sort of injury to the oviduct. Egg binding is a serious emergency, and the hen can die if she cannot pass the egg. Typical symptoms of egg binding are a breeding hen that looks fluffed up, depressed, or has a noticeable swelling low in her abdomen. An egg-bound bird might repeatedly squat, stand in an unusual or wide-legged stance, and wiggle her tail frequently. She will sometimes look as though she is straining and might appear lame.

If you suspect your bird is having difficulty passing an egg, place her into a brooder set at about 90°F (32°C), or a pet carrier with heating pad, immediately. High humidity is very helpful in this situation, so run a hot-water vaporizer nearby or place a pan of steaming hot water next to the carrier. You can tent a towel between the carrier and the pan to direct the warm vapors toward the bird. Obviously, be extremely careful to keep the pan out of reach of the bird so it cannot be scalded or burned. You can also place a bit of KY Jelly or mineral oil into her vent to help lubricate the area. If she does not pass the egg within a few hours, contact your veterinarian. The egg might have to be removed under anesthesia to save the hen's life.

Incubation Responsibilities

The parents share incubation duties, with the male doing mostly the day shift and the hen sitting at night. Sometimes they will both sit on the nest at the same time, especially as the eggs near hatching. In most cases, they will not begin incubation until the second egg is laid, so do not be concerned if you do not see them incubating the first egg immediately. Diamond Dove eggs hatch in about 12–13 days; Ringnecks hatch in 14–17 days. These are approximate times and might be affected by factors such as temperature, humidity, and parental nutrition. Depending on when the parents began incubation, the eggs might hatch within a few hours of each other or up to two days apart.

Raising the Chicks

Baby doves are called squabs. They are altricial, which means they hatch naked (except for some sparse down), blind, and helpless. The parents must feed them and keep them warm at all times, or they will not survive. Doves are usually

Depending on the species, dove squabs leave the nest between 10–30 days.

excellent parents and will wean their babies without assistance. (If something does go wrong and you are forced to step in, see the troubleshooting guide at the end of this chapter.)

For the first week or so of their lives, the parents feed the babies a substance known as crop milk. The crop is a food storage pouch that sits between the bird's esophagus and the first of its two stomachs. Doves and pigeons produce a unique high-protein substance in their crops that is a mixture of partially digested food and crop secretions, and this is what nourishes the squab. After about a week, the parents will start to feed a little seed or other foods to the chicks, who will usually leave the nest at 10–14 days or up to 30 days for larger, exotic species. During the time the parents are feeding the squabs, supply them with plenty of nutritious, high-protein foods, such as hard-boiled eggs or mealworms.

Hand-Rearing Chicks

If for any reason the parents are unable or unwilling to feed their squab, you might have to take over. Dove and pigeon squabs can be difficult to raise from day one because replicating crop milk can be hard. Roudybush manufactures a hand-rearing formula designed specifically for squabs, but it is not readily available in stores. You can order it through some veterinarians or on the Internet, or you can try one of the many brands of hand-rearing formulas developed for parrot chicks. The parrot formulas are not ideal for doves, but they will work if you are unable to get your hands on the squab diet quickly.

Parents will often chase youngsters away from the nest so that they can begin another clutch.

Troubleshooting Guide

Everything discussed so far about breeding assumes that all goes according to nature's plan and that the parents perform their duties without a hitch. Sometimes things do go wrong, however, and you are left to figure out how to prevent the problems from reoccurring. The following is a brief troubleshooting guide to help point you in the right direction.

- **Pair does not produce eggs.**
  - ✔ Same sex pair (two males)
  - ✔ Pair is not bonded
  - ✔ Poor nutrition
  - ✔ Old birds
- **Pair produces infertile eggs.**
  - ✔ Same sex pair (two females)
  - ✔ Poor nutrition
  - ✔ Poor mating technique, insufficient room in cage
  - ✔ Poor mating technique, improper (wobbly) perches

- **Fertile eggs that do not hatch.**
  - ✔ Improper incubation, allowing eggs to chill
  - ✔ Disease—transmitted from hen
  - ✔ Malnutrition
  - ✔ Genetic flaw (inbreeding)
  - ✔ Rough handling of eggs
- **Soft-shelled eggs.**
  - ✔ Calcium deficiency in hen
  - ✔ Old hen
- **Leg or beak deformities in squabs.**
  - ✔ Calcium or vitamin D deficiency
  - ✔ Improper (slippery) nesting materials
  - ✔ Injury in nest
  - ✔ Genetic flaw
- **Parents desert nest, destroy eggs, or kill babies.**
  - ✔ Disturbance in aviary, possible predator nearby
  - ✔ Displacement aggression due to overcrowding in aviary
  - ✔ Inexperienced parents (rare)

Doves have an entirely different feeding response from parrots and most other cage bird species. They take food from their parent's beaks, rather than gaping for the parents to feed them. Instead of attempting to put the formula into the squab's mouth, hold a spoonful of formula in front of the chick and gently dip its beak into the food. Once it senses the food, the bird will lap it up. You can also put the formula into a small paper cup and cut a little hole in the cup. Place the baby's beak into the hole, and it should start feeding vigorously. Allow the chick's crop to fill, but do not overfill it or the dove might aspirate the formula and suffocate.

Back to Nest

Often the parents will return to nest as soon as the babies are independent. If this happens, you will need to remove the first clutch of babies from the cage or the parents might start bullying them as they prepare for the next batch. Some pairs will continue to produce clutch after clutch, but this is dangerous for their health, especially for the hen. Producing eggs and caring for chicks is exhausting and puts great stress on the parents' bodies. If your birds do not stop on their own after two or at most three clutches, then remove the nesting materials or separate the birds if necessary.

Banding and Record Keeping

If you are serious and conscientious about raising doves, you will want to keep records and track your birds. At the very least, keep a file folder for each bird that lists age, description (color and sex), leg band number, genetics if known, and any health records. As you pair up your birds, you can also keep pair records such as clutches laid, hatch dates, color and sex of offspring, leg band numbers of offspring, and any other notes pertaining to the pair. A sturdy file box or binder works well, but some good computer programs designed for aviary management are available on the Internet. You will find these records invaluable as you add more birds to your collection. At some point you will not be able to depend on your memory to recall all of the history of each dove you own. If you decide to sell your birds, the new owner will also appreciate the background.

Leg Bands

As mentioned above, the best way to track the babies you have raised is with closed leg bands. These are small, solid rings that you slip over the squabs' legs when they are about a week old. As the babies grow, the band will not fit over the foot anymore, and so they cannot be put on or slipped off the leg. Leg bands are typically engraved with the year, a set of numbers or numbers and initials, and sometimes the state. If you purchase bands through some clubs or organizations, they will also engrave their initials or logo and keep your information on file. These bands are traceable, so someone purchasing one of your birds could identify you as the breeder by tracing the band number through the club. Untraceable bands are also available and can be purchased on the Internet and through many feed stores. These will have the same information as club bands. However, the information will help a buyer know only what year the bird was hatched, and possibly which state it was born in, because the band number is not recorded by any group.

To band the babies, gently grasp the three forward toes and bunch them together, then carefully slip the band over the forward toes and up onto the ankle. You can lubricate the squab's foot with petroleum jelly or a mild soap to make the band slide over easily. At this point, the back toe will be trapped under the band. Very gently grasp the toe and wiggle it free. You can use a toothpick to work the toe loose, but be very careful not to injure the chick. If you attempt to band the babies too early, the band will be too big and will likely slip off as the chick moves around. If you wait too long, you will not be able to fit the band over the chick's foot. Never under any circumstances try to force a band onto a baby that has grown too big, or you will injure the bird. Split bands are available that are put on with a special tool and can be placed onto a bird of any age. If you miss the window of opportunity to place a closed band onto the squabs, the split bands are an option. Try placing the closed bands when the babies are about six or seven days old. If the band is too big, just try again the following day. Baby doves grow amazingly fast, so check them daily.

OTHER DOVE SPECIES

With over 300 members of the family Columbidae, *describing more than a small cross section in a book of this length is obviously impossible. The great diversity and subtle beauty of doves make them a delight to behold, whether in the wild or in your own living room.*

Doves and pigeons range in size from the tiny Pygmy Ground Dove (*Columbina minuta*), which weighs about an ounce (29 g), to the impressive Victoria Crowned Pigeons (*Goura victoria*), which can stand over 2½ feet (75 cm) tall and weigh nearly 5 pounds (2.3 kg)! They live in every country of the world, except for Antarctica, and they thrive in cities, grasslands, and forests. The following are brief descriptions of some common and not-so-common members of the dove family that you might encounter.

Of course, common and uncommon are relative terms. Some of these birds are common in the wild, yet rare in captivity. There is also a wide variation in the availability of these birds depending on where you live. In general, those

Zebra Doves are aptly named for the barred effect on their chest. These quiet and adaptable doves do best in aviaries.

species that are readily available in aviculture are considered common, and those that are difficult to obtain are considered uncommon. Keep in mind that even the following "common" species will likely be unsuitable as house pets because they require more space or specialized care than Ringneck or Diamond Doves.

Common Species

Asian Dwarf Turtle Dove
(Streptopelia tranquebarica)

The Asian Dwarf Turtle Dove is also known as the Red Collared Dove or Red Turtledove. The males are a wine red color on their backs and wings with a grayish blue rump and head. A black ring circles the back of its neck, and its feet are dark reddish. The flight feathers are dark brown to charcoal. Females lack the red and are a brownish gray with charcoal flight feathers.

These small seed-eating doves are tolerant of cold weather and do best in flight cages. They are native to India and parts of Asia, although similar species range throughout much of Europe and northern Africa. They are available from U.S. breeders.

Cape Dove

(Onea capensis)

Also known as the Masked Dove or Namaqua Dove, the Cape Dove is an attractive, small dove ranging from western Saudi Arabia through most of southern Africa. The male has a characteristic black patch that extends from his forehead down through his breast, hence the common name Masked Dove. The female lacks the mask and is more plainly colored overall. The back and rump of both sexes is a brown, fading to a pale grayish white on the underparts. The tail and flight feathers are black.

These popular doves are about 9 inches (23 cm) long and weigh just less than 2 ounces (58 g). They are abundant in the wild and commonly available in aviculture.

Senegal Dove

(Streptopelia senegalensis)

The Senengal Dove is also known as the Laughing Dove due to its distinctive coo that sounds like human laughter. The wings, back head, and breast are a rusty brown, with gray blue or copper markings on its wings. The underparts are pale beige to nearly white. A bib of feathers under the chin are flecked with dark brown or black.

These birds are widely distributed throughout Africa, the Middle East, parts of Asia, and Australia. Although they prefer arid scrubland, they have adapted very well to living in villages and nesting on top of buildings. In captivity, they often become quite tame and trusting. Senegal Doves are approximately 11 inches (28 cm) long and weigh about 4 ounces (115 g).

Zebra Dove

(Geopelia striata)

The Zebra Dove is also known as the Peaceful Dove or Barred Ground Dove. As the name suggests, this small dove has black-and-white barring on its breast, throat, and neck, making it look a little like a feathered zebra. The back and rump are brown, and the underbody is white. The tail is black with white spotting.

Zebra Doves are found throughout Southeast Asia, Indonesia, northern Thailand, and parts of Australia. They are an introduced species in Hawaii. They are primarily terrestrial, spending most of their day on the ground, foraging for food. They are a popular aviary bird and heavily captured for the pet trade in Singapore. Despite this, Zebra Doves are adaptable and common across their native range. They are similar in size to the Diamond Dove.

Tambourine Dove

(Turtur tympanistria)

The Tambourine Dove is also known as the White-Breasted Wood Dove or Forest Dove. The male of the species has dark chocolate brown coloration extending from the top of his head down his back, fading to a slightly lighter brown on the rump. The wings have an olive green cast with a purple to bluish sheen. The hen is duller overall. The underbody is white on the male and pale gray on the hen.

Tambourines are shy birds and do not tame easily. They do best in planted aviaries. Their natural range is throughout sub-Saharan Africa, primarily in forested areas. They are about 8 inches (20 cm) long and weigh approximately 4 ounces (115 g).

White–Winged Dove
(Zenaida asiatica)

White-Wings are known for the characteristic white frontal wing band that is visible when the bird is perched. In flight, it appears as white wing patches. These medium-sized doves are mostly rust brown, fading to a grayish brown on their rump and underbody. A black patch is below the ear coverts, followed by coppery feathers.

Their native range is from Central America down through Chile and some Caribbean Islands, but they have expanded up through Mexico and into the southern United States. White-Winged Doves are considered an important pollinator and seed disperser for the saguaro cactus of the southwest. Their length is about 11 inches (28 cm), and weight is 4 ounces (115 g).

Inca Dove
(Columbina inca)

Inca Doves are native to the southwest United States and range down through Central America into Costa Rica. They are largely grayish brown, with dark edges on their feathers that give them a scalloped appearance. In flight, the underside of their wings shows a coppery rust color. Incas are somewhat shy but can become very tame with gentle handling. They are small birds, only about 8 inches (20 cm) long and weighing about an ounce (29 g).

Although they are found in most types of terrain, they seem to prefer populated and urban areas and are frequent visitors at bird feeders. Incas can be extremely aggressive with each other over food sources.

Mourning Dove
(Zenaida macroura)

Also known as the Carolina Dove, the Mourning Dove is a common fixture in yards across America. They are mostly terrestrial, spending much of the day poking around the ground in search of food. They enjoy frequent sunbaths and are quite trusting around humans. They are mostly brown with a long, pointed tail and black spots in the wings. In flight, their wings make a characteristic squeaking sound, and the tail shows white outer tail feathers. They are strong, fast fliers and can fly great distances when necessary in search of food or water.

This species is found throughout North and Central America, Cuba, and the Bahamas. They are medium-sized birds, measuring about 12 inches (30 cm) in length, and weighing 5 ounces (145 g).

Emerald Dove
(Chalcophaps indica)

Also known as the Green-Winged Dove, the beautiful Emerald Dove is common but secretive and shy. Colors can vary tremendously between individuals, but they are known for their wine red breast and throat with metallic green wings. Both sexes have a white forehead, but the male usually has a white shoulder patch that is absent or indistinct in the hens.

Emerald Doves occur in various subspecies throughout southern Asia, India, the Philippines, and parts of Australia and New Guinea.

Ringnecks are easy to breed and are available in over 40 color mutations.

Large doves and pigeons must be kept in aviaries with room to fly. Even some species of small doves do not do well in indoor cages.

Even if you have the space to build an aviary, do careful research on the needs and preferences of the species you wish to keep.

Diamond Doves are available in approximately 17 color mutations, although some are still quite rare.

Some species of doves are terrestrial, which means they spend most of their time scratching for food on the ground.

They typically feed on fallen fruit (especially figs) and seeds but will also eat insects. In aviaries, they require a lot of room to fly and do best in planted aviaries where they have vegetation to hide in for security.

They measure approximately 10 inches (26 cm) in length and weigh less than 4 ounces (115 g).

Uncommon Species

Victoria Crowned Pigeon
(Goura cristata)

Also known as the Blue-crowned pigeon or White-tipped crowned pigeon, the Victoria Crowned pigeon is a rare and beautiful bird found throughout northern New Guinea and nearby islands. These birds are mostly gray-blue, with a maroon breast and dark gray or black stripe running across the eye area. Their most striking feature is a large crest of white-tipped feathers on the head, which gives the birds the appearance of wearing an elegant crown.

These are the largest members of the *Columbidae* family, weighing in at about 4.5 pounds (2 kg), and standing about 30 inches (80 cm) in height. In the wild, they eat a variety of fruits, seeds, and insects.

Nicobar Pigeon
(Caloenas nicobarica)

The Nicobar pigeon is another bird with an impressive feather display. Nicobars have long neck feathers called hackles, which give the bird a maned appearance. Their plumage is generally a dark blue gray, with dark iridescent green on the wings and underparts. The tail is white, and there is a fleshy swelling at the base of the beak. They are about 15 to 17 inches (40–42 cm) in length, and weigh approximately one pound (.45 kg). They range from the Nicobar Islands of India all the way to the Solomon Islands in the Pacific, a distance of over 4,000 miles. Although widely distributed, they are rare and exist in small populations on various islands, making them extremely vulnerable to habitat destruction and hunting.

Recent DNA research indicates that the Nicobar pigeon is the closest living relative of the long extinct Dodo bird.

Mauritius Pink Pigeon
(Columba mayeri, also identified as *Nesoenas mayeri)*

This very rare bird has undergone a miraculous recovery thanks to a sustained and intensive management plan. In 1986, it was estimated that only about a dozen of these birds existed in the wild on the island of Mauritius, and a few hundred were in captive breeding programs around the world. The Mauritian government began an aggressive program of habitat protection, captive bird release, and management. The current wild population is somewhere between 300–400 individuals. These beautiful birds are light grayish pink on the breast and head, with darker pink on the underparts. The wings are a dark greenish brown, and the tail is reddish orange to brown. They weigh about 7 ounces (200 g), and are about 13 inches (34 cm) in length.

Bartlett's Bleeding-Heart Pigeon
(Gallicolumba criniger)

These beautiful, medium-size birds come from the forest of the Philippines. Their head and back are a metallic green with a purplish cast.

The upper breast is white, with a striking red patch. Their underparts are yellowish white to tan. They are 11–12 inches (28–30 cm) in length and weigh approximately 7 ounces (200 g). They are becoming increasingly rare in the wild due to habitat destruction and were recently upgraded to "endangered" status by the Convention on International Trade in Endangered Species (CITES). Although rare in aviculture, they are sometimes seen in zoos and at bird parks.

Polynesian Imperial Pigeon
(Ducula aurorae)

This rare and beautiful bird is found only on two islands: Tahiti and Makatea. It may even be extinct now on Tahiti. It was originally more widespread throughout several Polynesian islands, but habitat destruction and the introduction of new predators such as black rats have caused its extinction on most of the islands. On Makatea, much of the habitat was also destroyed, and the remaining birds populate just small areas of the island.

These are large pigeons with a broad wingspan and a prominent knob at the base of the bill. The head and underparts are a light silvery gray, with a dark bronze-green on the wings and back. They are approximately 18 inches (46 cm) in length, and weigh a little over one pound (.45 kg). In the wild, they are found in dense forests where they feed on a variety of fruit trees.

Polynesian Ground Dove
(Gallicolumba erythroptera)

These medium-size doves are critically endangered and very rarely seen. Although they were once found throughout much of Polynesia, they are now limited to the island of

Conservation Efforts

Many beautiful species of doves and pigeons (and countless other species of birds and animals) are fighting an uphill battle to survive in the face of habitat destruction and predation. Conservationists do what they can to introduce management plans and captive breeding programs but, unfortunately, they are not always successful. Other times, such as in the case of the Mauritius Pink pigeon, their efforts do pay off and a species is saved. That, of course, is a goal we should all strive to support.

Tenararo and possibly some remote and uninhabited forested islets. Habitat destruction, hunting, and the introduction of cats and rats to the islands have all played a part in decimating the population. In addition, these birds live on small islands that are vulnerable to storm damage, and populations can be wiped out in a single fierce storm.

The sexes are dimorphic, with the males more brightly colored. Males are mostly black with a white throat and face, and are suffused with a reddish-purple coloring on their backs and shoulders. The females are dark gray with grayish-white face and throat, and dull reddish feathers throughout their chest. Both sexes are approximately 10–11 inches (26–29 cm) in length, and weigh approximately 6 ounces (174 g).

In the wild, these doves eat a varied diet of fruits, seeds, green leaves, plant buds, and insects such as caterpillars. As their name implies, they spend much of their time foraging on the ground, and live mostly in dense shrubs underlying coconut trees and other vegetation.

COLOR MUTATIONS AND GENETICS

Mutations are genetic faults that occur naturally and randomly. In birds, mutations most commonly show as changes in feather color due to missing or altered pigmentation. Color mutations can be subtle or dramatic, affecting overall feather color or creating different patterns of color compared to normal birds.

Because many color variations are attractive and unusual, fanciers often breed their birds selectively to establish bloodlines that carry these traits. Some of these traits are dominant, which means that if either parent carries the pure gene, the offspring will look like the parents. Other genes are recessive, and the offspring will display the trait only if they receive the gene from both parents. Certain genes are sex-linked, which means they can display in some offspring, depending on the sex of the offspring and which parent passed along the recessive gene.

Color mutations occur randomly in nature, but breeders often work to establish these variations in a bloodline.

Genetics Basics

Genetics can get pretty complicated, but here are some simple examples for a single trait.

1. If both parents carry only a dominant gene (D) for the trait, then D + D = D. This means that all babies will grow up to look like the parents, and the offspring will carry only the dominant genes.

2. If one parent carries the dominant gene (D) and another carries a recessive gene (R) for the trait, then D + R = Dr. In this case, the offspring will all look like the parents, but the babies will carry both the the dominant and the recessive genes.

3. If both parents *display* the same recessive gene for the trait, then R + R = R. The offspring will look just like the parents and will carry only the recessive genes.

4. In sex-linked mutations, usually some of the female offspring will display recessive characteristics inherited from the father. Male offspring can carry the recessive gene but will not display the recessive trait unless they receive another copy of the recessive gene from their mother. Interestingly, in humans the exact opposite occurs. Male children can display recessive traits (such as male pattern baldness) that are passed on by their mothers, while female children can carry the trait but not display it.

5. In codominant mutations, both genes can express themselves, sometimes creating visual patterns that neither of the parents display or directly carry. In doves, some of the codominant genes become lethal to the offspring when passed on by both parents. This is one reason why genetics should be carefully studied and conscientiously applied when breeding mutations.

Genetics might sound pretty straightforward up to this point, but it becomes a lot more confusing when both parents carry hidden (recessive) genes, or you are breeding mutations to mutations. The simple charts on pages 87 and 91 will perhaps give you a better understanding of how these combinations work. At this point, there are fewer mutations and no sex-linked colors found in Diamond Doves, so their genetics are a bit simpler to understand.

Diamond Dove Genetics

Diamond Doves are now found in approximately 17 color mutations, although some are still quite rare. The normal, or wild color is called blue, and this is the dominant gene. Other colors include silver, cinnamon, red, ultra red, brilliant, yellow, ocher, and peach. In addition, feather patterns such as pied, white tails, and white rump are mixed with some of these colors. Brief color descriptions follow.

You can substitute any color mutation in place of yellow. Percentages are based on an average of clutches and might not exactly represent each clutch. Th chart on page 87 illustrates just a few simple combinations. Please note the possible combinations are practically endless, especially with breeding pairs that carry multiple mutations.

Silver mutation: A light silvery gray color. No dark edging on wing dots or flight feathers. First known mutation.

Cinnamon mutation: Displays a wide variety of rusty or red brown colors, ranging from pale to dark depending on the individual. No black edging on primary feathers.

Red mutation: A variation of the cinnamon mutation. Bright rusty-colored upper body with silvery white underparts. Females show more red than the males. No back edging and very little gray.

Ultra red mutation: Another cinnamon variant. Mostly white, with little or any gray. Vivid rust color on primary flight feathers. Females have more bright rust on their backs, neck, and head.

Brilliant mutation: Mostly white with a light gray cast. Some birds will show a faint tinge of color from the parental mutation. For example, brilliants born to a cinnamon parent might appear as pale pinkish white.

Yellow mutation: A relatively new mutation. They are a light honey or straw color with lighter underparts. Color is distributed over the

Displayed Color and Genetic Composition* in Diamond Doves

Male Parent	Female Parent	Male Offspring	Female Offspring
Wild (BB)	Wild (BB)	100% Wild (BB)	100% Wild (BB)
Wild (BB)	Wild (Bb)	100% Wild (50% BB; 50% Bb)	100% Wild (50% BB; 50% Bb)
Wild (BB)	Yellow (bb)	100% Wild (Bb)	100% Wild (Bb)
Wild (Bb)	Wild (BB)	100% Wild (50% BB; 50% Bb)	100% Wild (50% BB; 50% Bb)
Wild (Bb)	Wild (Bb)	75% Wild; 25% Yellow (25% BB; 50% Bb; 25% bb)	75% Wild; 25% Yellow (25% BB; 50% Bb; 25% bb)
Wild (Bb)	Yellow (bb)	50% Wild; 50% Yellow (50% Bb; 50% bb)	50% Wild; 50% Yellow (50% Bb; 50% bb)
Yellow (bb)	Wild (BB)	100% Wild (Bb)	100% Wild (Bb)
Yellow (bb)	Wild (Bb)	50% Wild; 50% Yellow (50% Bb; 50% bb)	50% Wild; 50% Yellow (50% Bb; 50% bb)
Yellow (bb)	Yellow (bb)	100% Yellow (bb)	100% Yellow (bb)

*B = blue/wild gene (dominant); b = yellow gene (recessive)
Any other single color trait can be substituted for yellow with the same results.

shoulders, backs, wings, and rump in a distinctive saddle pattern.

Ocher mutation: Combines yellow and cinnamon to produce a bird with a deep rust beige saddle, with dark red on the primaries. Underparts are gray with no black edging.

Peach mutation: A variation of yellow combined with silver. Shows the saddle pattern, but the color is a peachy beige. This mutation is new and very rare.

Pied mutation: Manifests as patchy spots of white feathering. The amount of white varies greatly among individuals. Pied mutations are currently showing up only on top of normal blue (wild) coloration, although some birds show as more brown gray than blue gray.

Ringneck genetics are quite complicated, with sex-linked and codominant traits appearing.

Careless breeding can introduce lethal genes that prevent eggs from hatching or kill birds after they are hatched.

A few color mutations in Zebra Doves have appeared in the wild. All white birds and dilute colors were reported in wild birds in Hawaii.

Always keep careful breeding records. Your system can be as simple as a spiral bound notebook, or as elaborate as one of the many bird breeder computer software programs available on the Internet.

Whatever path you choose, either as a single pet owner or a serious breeder, always take the time to appreciate and enjoy your bird(s).

White tail and white rump mutations: Can manifest in any of the previously discussed colors, including wild. The mutations that cause white tail and white rump are the same, and the only difference is the amount of white displayed. White tails are completely white on the tail and rump. White rumps are predominantly white throughout the tail and rump but can display gray or other pigments in varying degrees.

Ringneck Dove Genetics

The Ringneck Dove is available in over 40 color mutations, including white, albino, ivory, blond, rosy, pied, and tangerine, among others. Ringneck genetics are a little more complicated, because some of the mutations are sex-linked traits and some are codominant. Some traits are dominant relative to other traits. In other words, there is a hierarchy of sorts. For example, normal wild coloration is dominant to everything. Blond is recessive to wild but is dominant to white, and so on. Blond and white are sex-linked traits, so they will manifest differently than the non-sex-linked mutations listed in the Diamond Dove chart. The chart on page 91 highlights some typical genetic combinations for Ringnecks. As with the previous chart, this is just a small representative sampling and barely scratches the surface of possible combinations.

Several wonderful sites on the Internet explain dove genetics in detail, and these will be helpful if you decide to move beyond simple breeding combinations. See "Information" for details.

There are far too many mutations of Ringnecks to list them all here. However, the following is a sampling of many of these beautiful birds.

White mutation: These birds are not a pure white but are a soft off-white. Undertail barring is still visible. Feet are dark red. No neck ring.

Albino mutation: True albino is pure white, completely lacking in color. Eyes are unpigmented, so they appear pink to red because blood vessels are visible. No neck ring.

Ivory mutation: Very light off-white, sometimes displays subtle grayish cast.

Blond mutation: A light fawn color. This mutation is not yet recognized by the American Dove Association (ADA).

Rosy mutation: Rose-colored back and wings, lavender gray head. Neck ring and tail bars are darker brown.

Pied mutation: Patches of white, especially on the back, shoulders, and top of wings. Amount of white varies with individual birds.

Tangerine mutation: Pink orange back and wings, grayish white flight feathers and neck ring. Reduced tail barring.

Tangerine pearled mutation: Pink orange back. Flight feathers and neck ring are off-white. Minimal barring on tail.

Orange mutation: Orange brown coloration on back, rump, and wings. Head feathers lighter. Light gray flight feathers and neck ring.

Fawn mutation: Similar to wild color but much softer. Pinkish brown head, back, wings, and rump, medium gray flight feathers. Neck ring is charcoal to black.

Frosty mutation: Soft bluish gray with dark neck ring. Tail feathers white to light gray. Bill has dark stripe at end.

Frosty ice mutation: Similar to frosty but much lighter, nearly white with gray flecks.

Pink mutation: Very soft pinkish white. No tail barring or neck ring.

Cream pied mutation: Soft beige and white bird with medium gray brown neck ring.

Displayed Color and Genetic Composition* in Ringneck Doves

Male Parent	Female Parent	Male Offspring	Female Offspring
Wild (WW)	Wild (WW)	100% Wild (WW)	100% Wild (WW)
Wild (WW)	Blond (b–)	100% Wild (Wb)	100% Wild (W–)
Wild (WW)	White (w–)	100% Wild (Ww)	100% Wild (w–)
Wild (Ww)	Wild (WW)	100% Wild (50% WW; 50% Ww)	50% Wild; 50% White (50% WW; 50% w–)
Wild (Ww)	White (w–)	50% Wild; 50% White (50% Ww; 50% ww)	50% Wild; 50% White (50% W–; 50% w–)
Rosy (rr)	Rosy (rr)	100% Rosy (rr)	100% Rosy (rr)
Rosy (rr)	Wild (WW)	100% Wild (Wr)	100% Wild (Wr)
Tangerine (TW)	Wild (WW)	50% Tangerine; 50% Wild (50% TW; 50% WW)	50% Tangerine; 50% Wild (50% TW; 50% WW)
Tangerine (TW)	Tangerine (TW)	25% Tangerine Pearl; 50% Tangerine; 25% Wild (25% TT; 50% TW; 25% WW)	25% Tangerine Pearl; 50% Tangerine; 25% Wild (25% TT; 50% TW; 25% WW)
Frosty (FW)	Wild (WW)	50% Frosty; 50% Wild (50% FW; 50% WW)	50% Frosty; 50% Wild (50% FW; 50% WW)
Frosty (FW)	Frosty (FW)	25% Wild; 50% Frosty; 25% Dead in Shell (25% WW; 25% FW; 25% FF—Lethal)	25% Wild; 50% Frosty; 25% Dead in Shell (25% WW; 25% FW; 25% FF—Lethal)

*W = wild gene (dominant); b = blond gene (sex-linked); w = white gene (sex-linked); r = rosy gene (recessive); T = tangerine gene (codominant); F = frosty gene (codominant); – = no gene present due to sex-linkage

Although these descriptions are very brief, they will give you a glimpse of the amazing ranges of colors now available in domestic Ringnecks. Keep in mind that dove colors are very soft and muted compared with some other species of birds, but they are beautiful nonetheless. This very quiet and understated appeal is one reason doves are so popular.

Periodicals

Bird Talk/Birds USA
P.O. Box 6050
Mission Viejo, CA 92690
(949) 855-8822
www.animalnetwork.com

Bird Times
7-L Dundas Circle
Greensboro, NC 27407
(336) 292-4047
www.birdtimes.com

The AFA Watchbird
2208 "A" Artesia Boulevard
Redondo Beach, CA 90278

Organizations

American Dove Association
The *Dove Line* Newsletter
www.doveline.com

American Federation of Aviculture
P.O. Box 7312
North Kansas City, MO 64116
(816) 421-2473
www.AFAbirds.org

Association of Avian Veterinarians
P.O. Box 811720
Boca Raton, FL 33481
(561) 393-8901
www.aav.org

International Dove Society
3013 Tarpey Avenue
Texas City, TX 77590
www.internationaldovesociety.com

Helpful Web Sites

Diamond Dove Page by Jeff Downing
www.DiamondDove.com

The Dove Page by Wade Oliver
www.dovepage.com

Wilmer Miller's Web Page
www.RingneckDove.com

Manufacturers and Suppliers

Brinsea Products
3670 S. Hopkins Avenue
Titusville, FL 32780
(407) 267-7009
(incubators, brooders, egg candlers)

Celera AgGen
1756 Picasso Avenue
Davis, CA 95616
(800) 995-2473
(DNA testing and registry)

Corner's Limited
841 Gibson
Kalamazoo, MI 49001
(800) 456-6780
www.cornerslimited.com
(cages)

Humidaire Incubator Co.
217 West Wayne Street
New Madison, OH 45346
(937) 996-3001
(incubators)

Kaytee Products, Inc.
521 Clay Street
Chilton, WI 53014
(800) 669-9580
www.kaytee.com
(bird diets and hand rearing formula)

L&M Bird Leg Bands
P.O. Box 2943
San Bernardino, CA 92406
(909) 882-4649
(bird leg bands)

L'Avian Pet Products
Highway 75 S
P.O. Box 359
Stephen, MN 56757
(800) 543-3308
(L'Choice bird diets)

Lyon Electric Co.
2765 Main Street
Chula Vista, CA 91911
(619) 585-9900
www.lyonelectric.com
(incubators)

Pretty Bird International, Inc.
5810 Stacy Trail
P.O. Box 177
Stacy, MN 55079
(800) 356-5020
www.prettybird.com
(hand-rearing diets)

Prevue Pet Products, Inc.
224 N. Maplewood Avenue
Chicago, IL 60612
(800) 243-3624
(pet and breeding cages)

Rolf C. Hagen U.S.A. Corp.
50 Hampden Road
Mansfield, MA 02048
(800) 225-2700
www.pubnix.net/~mhagen
(various bird products, seed diets)

Roudybush Inc.
3550 Watt Avenue, Suite 8
Sacramento, CA 95821
(800) 326-1726
www.roudybush.com
(Roudybush bird diets, squab formula)

Stromberg's
P.O. Box 400
Pine River, MN 56474
(218) 587-2222
www.info@strombergschickens.com
(supplies and birds)

Valentine Inc.
4259 S. Western Boulevard
Chicago, IL 60609
(800) 438-7883
(galvanized wire, cage building supplies)

About the Author

Gayle Soucek has been breeding and training birds for over 15 years. She has been recognized as a Certified Avian Specialist (C.A.S.) by the Pet Industry Joint Advisory Council. She is past president of the Midwest Avian Research Expo, the Midwest Congress of Bird Clubs, and the Northern Illinois Parrot Society. Gayle is a current member of the American Federation of Aviculture, the Society of Parrot Breeders and Exhibitors, and the African Parrot Society.

Gayle has written several books and articles, which have appeared in numerous magazines. She and her husband live in the Chicago area and currently share their home with macaws, cockatoos, Amazons, Quakers, several types of African parrots, parrotlets, a few other assorted parrot species, and one very tolerant dog. Her special areas of interest are avian health, nutrition, and captive breeding.

Cover Photos

Front cover: B. Everett Webb; back cover, inside front and inside back cover: E.J. Peiker

Photo Credits

Norvia Behling: pages 5, 21 (bottom), 28 (top left), 29; E.J. Peiker: pages 3, 4, 16, 17, 20, 21 (top), 24, 32, 36, 37, 40, 44, 57, 60, 72, 73, 76, 84, 88, 89; B. Everett Webb: pages 8, 9, 12, 13, 25, 28 (top right; bottom), 33, 45, 49, 52, 53, 56, 64, 65, 68, 69, 77, 80, 81, 85

© Copyright 2006 by Barron's Educational Series, Inc.

All inquiries should be addressed to:
Barron's Educational Series, Inc.
250 Wireless Boulevard
Hauppauge, NY 11788
www.barronseduc.com

ISBN-13: 978-0-7641-3232-2
ISBN-10: 0-7641-3232-6

Library of Congress Catalog Card No. 2005050023

Library of Congress Cataloging-in-Publication Data
Soucek, Gayle.
    Doves : everything about purchase, care, nutrition, and breeding / Gayle A. Soucek.
        p. cm. — (A Complete pet owner's manual)
    Includes index.
    ISBN-13: 978-0-7641-3232-2
    ISBN-10: 0-7641-3232-6
        1. Pigeons. I. Title. II. Series.

SF465.S587   2006
636.5'96—dc22   2005050023

Printed in China
9 8 7 6 5 4 3 2 1